Hear Me Out

Hear Me Out

True Stories of Teens Educating and Confronting Homophobia

A Project of Planned Parenthood of Toronto

Second Story Press

Library and Archives Canada Cataloguing in Publication

Hear me out : true stories of teens educating and confronting homophobia /
Teens Educating and Confronting Homophobia (T.E.A.C.H.).

Originally presented as part of T.E.A.C.H.'s presentations to schools: Safely out.
ISBN 1-896764-87-8

1. Coming out (Sexual orientation) 2. Homophobia in high schools--Ontario--
Toronto. 3. Gay teenagers--Ontario--Toronto.
I. Teens Educating and Confronting Homophobia (Youth group)
II. Title: Safely out.

HQ76.45.C32T67 2004   306.76'6   C2004-905266-7

Planned Parenthood is a member of the United Way of Greater Toronto

Edited by Frances Rooney
Front cover photograph and front cover design by Ariel P. Vente
Text design by L. McCurdy and P. Rutter
Typesetting by P. Rutter

Printed and bound in Canada

*Second Story Press gratefully acknowledges the support of the Ontario Arts Council
and the Canada Council for the Arts for our publishing program. We acknowledge
the financial support of the Government of Canada through the Book Publishing
Industry Development Program, and the Government of Ontario through the
Ontario Media Development Corporation's Ontario Book Initiative.*

Canada Council
for the Arts

Conseil des Arts
du Canada

ONTARIO ARTS COUNCIL
CONSEIL DES ARTS DE L'ONTARIO

Published by
Second Story Press
720 Bathurst Street, Suite 301
Toronto, ON
M5S 2R4
www.secondstorypress.on.ca

Acknowledgments

This collection was anthologized by a special
editorial committee comprised of: Nadia Bello, Susan Flynn,
Hazelle Palmer, Rico Rodriguez and Ariel Vente.
Story editing by Rico Rodriguez and Nadia Bello.

Dedication

This anthology is dedicated to the T.E.A.C.H. volunteers
whose stories fill the pages of this special collection; and to all
T.E.A.C.H. volunteers past, present and future whose courage to
speak out makes it possible for others to listen, opening
their hearts and minds.

Table of Contents

Foreword

We all know growing up is filled with life-changing experiences. Puberty, sexual readiness and dating, developing our individual style, coping with relationships, with parents and friends all contribute to the roller coaster of experiences that help form who we are and who we will become. Discovering in the midst of all these shifts that you are attracted to people of your own gender or that you are not the same gender inside as outside can send the roller coaster off course.

Hear Me Out is a collection of unique and personal stories by volunteers with Toronto's Teens Educating and Confronting Homophobia (T.E.A.C.H.), a peer-based program run by Planned Parenthood of Toronto (PPT) to educate and change negative attitudes about gay, lesbian, queer, bisexual, transsexual and transgendered people. From coming out to finding love, dealing with violence to internal homophobia, these voices speak to the specific difficulties of growing up "queer."

When I was in high school I can't remember any deep and challenging discussions with my friends about homosexuality. The only time it came up, really, was when we'd yell "fag" down the hall after a boy we didn't like or found effeminate. On reflection, the cruelty and homophobia are clear, but thirty years ago, these comments were just considered to be part of high-school life. I can't imagine what it must have been like for youth who were questioning their orientation and scared by our bullying.

The stories in this collection tell us very clearly what it is like: isolating, emotionally draining, frightening, sometimes empowering and supporting. It's hard to tell how much has really changed over the years. Are school environments today any safer for queer youth? Are name-calling, bullying, taunting, queer-bashing and violence still prevalent? Is there support for open discussions among youth about sexual orientation that challenges stereotypes, myths and perceptions?

About T.E.A.C.H.

T.E.A.C.H. was established in 1993 to raise awareness of these issues. Founded at a time when queer discrimination in high schools in the east end of Toronto was escalating, the program created a peer-based framework to challenge youth about their attitudes to gays, lesbians, bisexuals and transgender/transsexuals. PPT has run the program since 1997. We have very limited staff resources, some support from United Way of Greater Toronto and the Ontario Trillium Foundation and about twenty-five incredible volunteers each year, all truly committed to challenging homophobia and creating safer school and community environments.

When we adopted the program from East End Community Health Centre, T.E.A.C.H. was not like PPT's other programs, the core of which are sexual and reproductive health education and clinical services. However, because the effects of homophobia on self-esteem, body image and sexuality, and their link to violence are so clear, particularly for youth the connection to healthy sexuality is undeniable. There were also practical reasons for the adoption. We could make T.E.A.C.H. available to city-wide audiences and use our strong reputation for fundraising to advocate for the increased financial resources that could stabilize the program. And with T.E.A.C.H. as part of our PPT programs, we could better diversify our client base to reach more queer-identified youth. Planned Parenthood of Toronto was ready for the challenge; was everyone else ready for T.E.A.C.H.?

Linking anti-homophobia to healthy sexuality has been our greatest stumbling block. Some people and funders believe that social or community-based services should be compartmentalized or specialized, ought to focus, for example, on sexual health, anti-violence or anti-homophobia education. Not all three. However, we approach our work at Planned Parenthood of Toronto from a holistic perspective, easily connecting how the social determinants of health directly impact our capacity to live well and be healthy. It is impossible for us to speak about healthy sexuality and not consider how that affects anyone who is lesbian, gay, bisexual or transgender/transsexual (LGBT). How could we argue for the right of informed decision making when we do not include the right to disclose one's sexual orientation without fear of bias or judgment? How could we proudly support pro-choice values and beliefs and not recognize the barriers that exist for LGBT people to exercise choice in their daily lives?

T.E.A.C.H. is helping to break down those barriers or at least, as its name implies, is confronting the cause. Each year T.E.A.C.H. volunteers undergo a seven-session training program to equip them for the questions and reactions they will face when speaking to classrooms filled with young and eager minds. The volunteers, who identify as gay, lesbian, bisexual, transgender and straight allies, and who range in age from fifteen to twenty-three, share their own personal stories. This approach has proved to be successful in helping youth to make connections with their audience and to resonate with other youth who may be questioning their orientation. Volunteers are also trained to support the youth when conducting workshops. These support volunteers assist in facilitation, help debrief workshops and give feedback to PPT's program staff. Although some participants still refuse to be engaged or to shift their thinking, evaluations from these sessions have recorded definite changes in perceptions and attitudes by many of the participants.

About the anthology

Not all the stories featured here are about growing up or high-school life per se. What they have in common is that they vividly demonstrate how difficult it is to be different at any stage of life. They show that discovering sexual orientation or gender preference comes at an unimaginable price. These stories tell of the process of coming out — telling family, friends and acquaintances. The writers recount how vulnerable a person is to the reactions of others. We read how hard it is to find support and community — are there others like me? Am I alone? And the stories allow us, the readers, to witness these young people's love interests: the secret crushes, first loves, Internet love, dating and marriage.

Then there's homophobia. Homophobia from family members, friends or strangers, at home, at a bar, at work or at school. Perhaps worst is internalized homophobia, the self-loathing and doubt that are all too common. Racism, sexism, ageism, classism and ablism, from the straight and queer communities alike, increase a person's marginalization. Cultural and religious values and beliefs cloak the LGBT community further, making being queer a complex and profoundly isolating identity.

Homophobia and transphobia can be demonstrated in many ways: outright fear of homosexuals and transgender/ transsexuals, taunting and name-calling, gay-bashing and other forms of hate violence. The torture and murder of twenty-one-year-old Matthew Shepard because he was gay brought the issue of hate violence out of the closet in the United States and onto the world's stage. Such violence wasn't new, but this case proved further that despite slowly changing social consciousness about homophobia and its impact on the quality of life for homosexuals and heterosexuals, being LGBT puts your life at risk.

For many of us doing anti-homophobia/transphobia work,

incidences like Shepard's re-affirm our belief that reaching individuals earlier and throughout their formative years helps to prevent the escalation of homophobia to hate violence. In an interview on CBC radio following Shepard's murder, Canadian lawyer Barbara Findlay commented how such an escalation can occur: "It starts with what they get away with before that stage when they were able to go out with a baseball bat and a tire iron. How many times did they drive down a main street ... and call someone a fag? How often did they ... get away with a whole range of smaller ... mindless, little, childhood pranks? And even before that, the most common epithet in the public school system is 'faggot.' Children call each other faggot ... [when] they only know it means something very, very bad.... Our children ... are schooled in the kind of attitude which is consistent with activities like this."

Homophobia, like other forms of discrimination, is so systemic that significant change is difficult to obtain and attempts at change often meet with harsh resistance. When issues like same-sex marriage are debated, we get to see people's views on homosexuality and homophobia become vocal and public. Homosexuality, it seems, is okay so long as it stays closeted.

Hear Me Out!

Hear Me Out is about letting people and their stories out of the closet; it is about sharing personal, sometimes intimate moments that demonstrate how homophobia hurts *and* how being different is empowering.

This is a collection that is as diverse as its storytellers, and readers will find unique circumstances and perhaps the familiarity of moments that show that there are others like them.

The real challenge is for all of us who read this anthology to face our own homophobia and take a leadership role in demanding personal and systemic change. We need to embrace and celebrate differences all the time, not just at particular times of year. If we're committed to equal rights then we must support equal rights for everyone. We must understand that when we advocate for safer schools, it's about creating learning environments that are free of *all* forms of discrimination, including homophobia and transphobia, name-calling, bullying, bashing and hate violence.

T.E.A.C.H. volunteers have been going into schools for over ten years telling their stories. Welcome to this small sample of what they have to say.

Hear them out!

Hazelle Palmer
Executive Director
Planned Parenthood of Toronto
May 2004

Program Co-ordinator's Intro

The title of one of the stories in this anthology is "This Is Not a Coming Out Story" — and it's not. Neither is this anthology yet another "coming out" book. Rather it is a reclaiming, reshaping and recognition of the role of personal storytelling as a means of educating around, sharing and healing the experiences of homophobia, transphobia and heterosexism. Storytelling remains at the heart of the workshops facilitated by T.E.A.C.H. volunteers. In all the submissions in this anthology, you will find elements of "traditional" coming out stories that tell what it's like to come out to our parents, our friends, our families, ourselves. The stories that T.E.A.C.H. facilitators tell affirm that while not always a positive experience, coming out remains a lifelong experience — that no matter our sexual identity, everyone is always "coming out" as something. Every time we speak, take a stand or form an opinion, we come out. All the stories here speak to coming out in the broadest possible sense: a coming out of self; a coming out that includes all kinds of identities around sexuality, race, education, privilege, awareness, celebration.

As the current co-ordinator of T.E.A.C.H., my history with the program is a long and complicated one. I joined T.E.A.C.H. at the age of nineteen, struggling with my identity, my body, my place in the world. I spent three years as a peer facilitator, alternately loving the work because I could see the impact of T.E.A.C.H. workshops and of my story on other youth and hating it because of the toll anti-homophobia education took on my mind and soul. After a year away, I rejoined the program as staff, first as an assistant and eventually becoming program coordinator, all by the age of twenty-four. In many ways, my experience with T.E.A.C.H. has shaped my early adult life.

I continue to be so invested and passionate about anti-homophobia education, and the work of T.E.A.C.H. in particular, because homophobia remains one of the most virulent and widespread forms of hatred in our society. It is because homophobia is born of and breeds racism, sexism and class bias. It is because people *learn* to hate when they are very young and because the minds and hearts of youth are both the battleground and mirror of the society we live in. It is because youth are denied agency on many grounds, especially sexual ones, having our identities and experiences ignored, condemned, made illegitimate. It is because people have lost their homes, been made destitute, and been abused, maimed, criminalized and institutionalized, erased and killed for not only not being heterosexual but for being perceived as non-heterosexual. Because "that's so gay" is so acceptable. And finally, because there's nothing that I've written that does not apply to women, immigrants, people of color, First Nations peoples, poor people — anyone who's ever known what it's like to be systemically excluded and marginalized.

For queer and trans-identified youth in particular, the tensions inherent in some of these pieces are a reflection of how hard and yet at the same time how empowering it is to use personal storytelling as a means of education and reaching out. The stories of T.E.A.C.H. facilitators put a human face to otherwise dogmatic and abstract ideas of sexuality. They take away the comfort of "I was raised to think this way" about gay people or

"I've never known anyone who was a lesbian." Well, now you do, and guess what? We like the same kind of ice cream and have the same taste in music. That is the power of peer education and those are the kinds of bridges personal storytelling can build. And I believe that stories are one of the most powerful, but underused, tools available to youth for self-preservation, identity and empowerment.

Survival, transformation, hiding, realization and relationships are just some of the themes that run through this anthology. Who cannot relate to stories with these themes? Who does not, consciously or unconsciously, use stories as a way to experience and interpret the worlds around and inside us? Everyone has stories to tell, even though some of us believe we don't. I hope this anthology gives you voice and hope to be able tell your own stories.

Nadia Bello
T.E.A.C.H. Program Co-ordinator
May 2004

✦✦✦

Reconciliation

Amina Jabbar

My name is Amina. *I started telling this story at T.E.A.C.H. workshops just recently. Although I've been with T.E.A.C.H. for four years now, I didn't come out to myself until about two years ago. Being able to tell this story was for me about reconciling my cultural and religious identities with my sexuality. My cultural and religious identities tend to reinforce each other; they're so closely intertwined that I sometimes have a hard time distinguishing one from the other. I am a South-East Asian person who is Muslim. My identities are typically at odds with being queer-identified. Growing up, I felt like they would team up just to gang up on my sexuality. That battle and reconciliation is really the centrepiece of my story.*

I was born in Saudi Arabia, far, far away, as I suppose it seems to many people. My father worked there as a doctor on a fairly lucrative eight-year contract. I lived in a way that didn't seem as odd or off-kilter as people usually think it must have been. My best imaginary friend was Snuffy from Sesame Street and Bionic Woman was my hero. Yup, I grew up within a pretty average household.

When my father's contract was up, we packed our belongings and went to the United States of America. As an eight-year-old, moving into the inner city of Chicago was one hell of a shock to my system. I had lived in a world that was virtually all Muslim and mostly Arab. That was my bubble and I had no conception of anything that existed outside of that. All of the sudden, there were so many people of different races and religions and backgrounds, all of which I didn't realize existed until I moved. Although Chicago was a very diverse city, I did not fit in. My thick accent was a problem; I didn't have the greatest working knowledge of English and I was a really fat kid. All of that meant that I didn't make a lot of friends.

But change was in the cards for me.... In seventh grade, things turned around completely. I applied and got into Whitney Young Magnet High School near the core of downtown Chicago. My friends and I joked that the school just picked all the maladjusted, screwed-up kids from the around the city and stuck them together. My parents, not completely aware of what the school was like, only let me go because it was a school for gifted students. For my mother in particular, education was of the utmost importance, and my parents felt that Whitney Young presented the best opportunity for me. The teachers at the school felt it was their duty to encourage and cultivate diversity of all forms. They constantly reminded us, almost like a mantra, that we as students could choose any path we desired. At Whitney Young there were many clubs and we were encouraged to join at least one of them.

At the time I was beginning to question my sexuality. Whitney had an LGBTQ–Straight Alliance and I was thinking about joining it because I felt that it would be a comfortable place to ask the questions I had within me. I felt it would be the right place for me. This was precipitated by something that happened at school.

A few weeks before I joined the Alliance, I gave myself a bit of a jolt. There was this guy, Ryan, who was the class heartthrob. Personally, I couldn't have cared more or less about him. He had started going out with Lily, a girl from our class. One day between classes, I was walking with a couple of friends to my next class. I looked up and saw Ryan and Lily holding hands and a shot of jealousy ran up my spine. At first, my reaction was a little puzzling. I knew I didn't care for Ryan. But then I realized, "OhmiGod, I have a crush on Lily."

When I joined the LGBTQ–Straight Alliance, my intention was to gain some perspective from other people. First, I wanted to know if other people had the same experiences. Then, if I felt comfortable, I thought to myself, I'd think about disclosing my own feelings. Most important, this was a place where I could get a range of opinions, because I certainly wasn't getting them from my parents.

As far as my parents were concerned, exploring one's sexuality was off limits. According to my parents, sexuality only existed within heterosexual marriage. They felt that holding on to this value was important to resist the American melting pot. They also felt it was crucial that their children retain the cultural and religious values they were raised with. In other words, I wasn't allowed to do anything my parents deemed Americanized/ Westernized. So I knew full well that if I ever asked to go to the homecoming dance my school held at the end of October, I was in for a good slap and a good yelling that'd last for days. I wasn't allowed to do most things that average teenagers were supposed to do. Going out to the movies with a bunch of friends — out of the question. Going to the mall to hang out — out of the question. Having platonic friendships with guys — out of the question. Boyfriends, sex and sexual orientation were topics not even on the radar. And if I did bring them up, I was set for another good yelling because they defined the pinnacle of Westernized Evil.

I remember watching TV with my father one afternoon. There was something on the news about LGBT rights. My father made a comment that he believed that being gay was a symptom of being exposed to Western culture. As far as he was concerned, Muslims could not be gay. If a Muslim was gay, well then, he/she was just not really Muslim. That was that and there was no real dialogue or conversation after my father stated his piece. He wouldn't have it any other way.

Oddly enough, I didn't get what I was looking for at the LGBTQ–Straight Alliance. If anything, it pushed me further back into the closet. At the group, I met people who were LGBTQ-identified and were out but none of them had the same struggle to reconcile their sexual orientation with culture and religion as I did. There weren't any South-East Asian women or Muslim women within the Alliance, let alone South-East Asian or Muslim women who were out. For me, the absence of other South-East Asian Muslim women within the group felt like I wasn't supposed to identify as anything but straight.

When I was in the middle of grade ten we moved again. My parents had grown weary of not living close to relatives. So we packed our bags and moved to Scarborough, Ontario, Canada, where we had lots of relatives. There I experienced a different kind of shock; not the kind I did when we moved to Chicago — shock with a different flavor. I remember my first day at Wilfrid Laurier Collegiate very vividly. By now I had lost most of my weight, so that couldn't be a problem anymore. I had lost my accent while living in Chicago, so that couldn't be a problem either. What shocked me was that the teachers and students decided to label me before they even got to know me. They did not even give me the chance to label myself. That day I had dressed as I would have on any other school day. I wore an oversized T-shirt, skater pants and a chain that hung from my wallet down to my knee. So I didn't think I looked particularly different from any of the other kids. Then I walked into my first class of the day, English, and I could have sworn my teacher's head turned 180 degrees. I was shocked; I couldn't figure out why. And I will never forget the major attitude I got from the students. They made me feel as if I had been silently declared the school dyke. Word was that it was my wardrobe that did the trick. It did not matter whether I was one or not. For the first time in my life, I was experiencing homophobia at school. So from the get-go my personal life was complicated.

This was very difficult for me because at that point I was questioning my sexuality even more. I didn't know anyone who was Muslim and LGBTQ. I didn't have the ability to try to find someone who was, either. So most of me came to the conclusion that being LGBTQ just wasn't in the cards for someone like me. What my father had said about being gay was also ever present in my mind, and I kept hearing the same sentiments from the twenty other family/friend households in our building. But nothing shocked me more about moving to Scarborough than to realize, much to my horror, that there was still a large number of people around who had no inkling of what gay really meant. They knew gay and dyke meant something derogatory. But a potted plant probably would've given a better answer about what being gay or a dyke really meant. With all the exposure I had at the LGBTQ–Straight Alliance in Chicago, the meaning of gay had been well integrated into my life in a positive way. I just knew that "some boys like boys and some girls like girls and some people like boys and girls." It was that simple.

Although I thought that as a Muslim woman I wasn't allowed to identify as LGBTQ, I felt it was all right for me to fight against homophobia and for rights. Near the end of high school, my principal wanted to organize a human rights conference at the school. She gave me the assignment to call a group called T.E.A.C.H. and book a speaker. While calling to book the speaker, I learned about T.E.A.C.H. I was excited about them coming to my school. But the conference my principal tried to pull together fell through not long after. In the end, I decided to join T.E.A.C.H. because I rationalized that that was the best way to fight homophobia.

I had a really rough time keeping my connection with T.E.A.C.H. from my dad. To him it would have been like collaborating with the enemy. My mom, on the other hand, knew about it all along. She wasn't one to care much about what I did anyway. My mother ... she's quite the liberal-minded lady. You wouldn't think that at first glance, seeing that she's an orthodox Muslim who proudly wears the hijab everywhere she goes. She was the one who taught me that for a woman getting an education "isn't a choice; it is a necessity." Within that lesson, she also taught me how to question everything, including religion.

I finished high school and managed to scrape enough cash together from working full-time in the summer to move away from my parents. I was going to go to the University of Toronto. Out of grip and sight of family, I could do my own thinking. I was paging through a magazine one day, and again, completely by accident, I stumbled onto an article about being LGBTQ and Muslim. I think I must have read the article from beginning to end at least thirty times. At the same time, though, the article seemed distant. I was irrationally worried someone had made it all up. I had to listen to an out Muslim woman speaking to really make it hit home. I rather randomly decided to go to a human rights conference on U of T campus. It was sort of like the ultimate thunderbolt in the sky, the sign I was waiting for. I don't know exactly what it was that made listening to her change everything for me. Maybe it was the fact that I needed to physically see her. Maybe what I heard made me realize that my father's convoluted value system had a stronger grip over my life than I thought. Maybe I simply needed the time. In the end, the reason didn't really matter. I got to that place in my life where I could finally identify as being queer.

I knew that was a sense of peace I couldn't afford to give up ever again.

✦✦✦

"Don't Deny It..."

Anna Penner

I remember the first time I heard about T.E.A.C.H.: A new friend suggested I join. Public speaking was something I had always enjoyed, one of the things that had made me happy at all points in my life. The possibility to speak to others about my experience, to give other people the education I had never been offered, was amazing. I went to an interview and was accepted into training in the fall of 2001. So many questions at T.E.A.C.H. read, "If you could change yourself, would you?" It's a complicated question, and has had different answers at different points. Would I have at one point? Yes.

I was sixteen. I was sitting in a Winnipeg basement with its gray carpet and gray chair. I was reading a copy of Teen People — the cool thing to read. I was trying so hard. "Ten Teens Who Will Change the World," was the headline. One of them was a lesbian, a girl not much older than myself. She had been scared. She had denied it. Through my tears her image blurred into my own. I knew. I couldn't deny it. I couldn't hide it. I was her.

In the same moment I knew I was gay, I knew I was homophobic. I didn't have the language for it; I didn't have any way to express it. I just knew that I was disgusted with myself. That I'd do anything I could to take back what I had just realized. If you had asked me on that day, I would have given anything for an easy answer that would have set things back according to plan. My plan. My parents' plan. My school's plan. My society's plan. I would have given anything, but there was nothing I could get in return. There are no pills. There is no therapy. There are no magic answers. I was so scared, and so many things came flooding back to me....

In fifth grade they played "lesbo tag." Whoever got tagged was a lesbian. A kind of irradicable form of the cooties, a word that can send the entire perilously framed society of a fifth-grade classroom tumbling. They called me a lesbian. It wasn't in those games of tag, where half the class was a lesbian at some point during lunch recess. It was when the new girl came — long hair, quiet, sulking, drawing in the margins of her notebook. She was different. I liked her. I called her my best friend and held her hand during recess. I called her my best friend; they called us lesbians. I was shocked. In the world of close friendships and half-heart necklaces, I was the one they singled out. I got scared. Instead of holding her hand, I ran from her.

When I learned, much later, the word "heterosexism," I could look back and apply it to my entire education: It wasn't that homosexuality was wrong, it just didn't exist. Sex education was about how to say no and about how to put a condom on a banana.

The biggest lie I had ever been told was that I would hit puberty and start being attracted to boys. In a chain reaction with blood on panties and changing bodies, I assumed it to be an infallible truth. But it didn't happen. Not then, not in that way. That isn't the sort of thing you admit in elementary school — I learned that eventually.

When I was in sixth grade our family moved to England for a year. The educational system is different, and as a result I was placed with students my own age but effectively a grade ahead. They were already talking about boys and bras, giggling in the locker room. I was strange in so many ways: the kid with an accent, the kid who just didn't understand. When I returned to Canada, it wasn't any better. It was as though, over the course of a year, everything I had ever known had changed. What had been acceptable a year ago wasn't anymore. I left a bunch of kids and I came back to a group of teenagers interested in makeup and boys. For years I thought that was what had made me different; as if during a year-long absence, I had missed some strange initiation, a rite of passage that would make these transformations logical.

A girls' school is a strange environment, a sort of reality buffer where makeup, parties and boys initially seem far away. In an all-girl environment in a coed world, it was okay for boys to be icky for a while longer. But there was television. There were movies. I remember going to my friend's house and seeing her walls postered with pictures of a smiling teenage celebrity. I was so confused. No, he wasn't cute. I didn't even know what I was supposed to be looking for, what I was supposed to see. I was the only one who still thought boys were gross. At some point, thinking that stopped being okay. I wondered for brief, scared moments, but forgot. I didn't want to know. I wanted to keep on waiting for those magical changes the puberty of three years ago had been intended to bring. I wanted to keep pretending that all I wanted was my female friends to be close friends, nothing more.

I fell head-over-heels for a girl. I watched her walk into my school on her first day there, and I just stared. She was beautiful, she was talented and she was different. She is still the biggest crush I've ever had, though she'll never know that. She made me realize I couldn't deny what I was feeling, and she made me realize that what I was feeling was more than friendship. As I blushed, stammered and stuttered my way through that crush, I realized that I was suddenly feeling all the things that everybody had always told me I would feel, but I was feeling these things for a girl.

So when I was sixteen, on New Year's Eve, I cried and resolved in my head to come to terms with my sexuality. I tried. I came out to my teddy bear a hundred times — making my heart pound and my breath stop to just try and say those words out loud. I searched the Internet; I found a group in Winnipeg. For the first time ever, I lied to my parents about where I was going. I walked into a room filled with shabby couches and young, gay men. I went twice before my parents realized I was lying about where I was going. They never did find out where I actually had been: I told them that it didn't matter, that I wasn't going back. And I didn't.

I lied. I made up crushes. I watched carefully and learned what made a boy "cute" or not. I got good at it, and I almost believed it. So when groups of giggling girls made lists of who they thought was a lesbian, I never made it onto those pages. I would offer my own suggestions or speculations, throw in a comment or two, but I never tried to stop them. Am I ashamed? In hindsight, yes. Was I then? No, just glad that my name wasn't written down. One of my friends came out to me, and I supported her. But I couldn't support myself. I couldn't even tell her then. It wasn't only about other people hating me anymore. It was about hating myself. Being disgusted. Being ashamed. Even when homophobia isn't directed at you, you see it and hear it every day. People calling each other names, hostile speculations about whichever celebrity happens to be called gay at the moment, rumors about unpopular classmates, whispers of, "That's so gay." And on television, in movies, in magazines, famous people beautifully paired like Barbie and Ken. It all screamed, "That's what's normal." Heterosexism is an undeniable reality of growing up in this society. And I internalized it all — made all those comments, all those games, all those opinions into my own shame.

I hated myself. My resolution to come to terms with my sexuality was almost forgotten. Instead, I decided it would just be a life-long secret: something I never told, something that nobody would ever need to know. If I could lie today, I could lie tomorrow. If I could do that, I could lie next week, next month, next year. I could spend my life pretending. I could be normal, or at least a passing imitation of it.

I hated myself. I hurt. I wanted that hurt to show. I cut my arms with razors. I scratched my hands. I hit my body. It wasn't pretty and I don't want this to be pretty. My teachers worried about the change, talked about family problems and made my mother cry. I was ashamed. So I didn't cut much anymore, at least not so they could see. I still hurt, though. Quietly and desperately, I hurt.

It hurts, even now, to remember. I want to forget, but I won't let myself. If I forget this, then I can forget why I do T.E.A.C.H., why homophobia in kids makes me so angry. I don't want to forget how it feels to be so young and so scared, so trapped in what people think is a carefree world. My mother still believes I never had any problems.

I couldn't hide. Not always, not forever. So I started counting the years, months and days until university. Until a different city with different people. Until I got away from all the people I was so scared of disappointing — except myself. The first time I remember counting down, it was two years and two months until university. It was a long wait. I thought everything would be perfect when I went to university, that it would be the answer to all of my problems. That it would be a community of creative, eclectic, understanding people who knew exactly what I had gone through. I built up some knowledge and some sense of the community from the Internet, a sort of preview of what I thought was to come. People who understood me telling their secrets to the online world. Websites and chat rooms, short-haired girls and flamboyant boys ... it's what I was looking for so it's what I found. I dreamed of the day when it would be my tangible reality, not just a faraway vision. One day I would meet these people. Just not today. They would welcome me with open arms into a peaceful, smiling community. I needed to believe in this unrealistic utopia. I needed to believe in the charms of a bigger city. In a way, I still do.

I came to the University of Toronto with a secretly gathered knowledge of what gayness awaited me — LGBTOUT, LGBYT, SEC (the University of Toronto Sexual Education and Peer Counselling Centre). Organizations with websites showing smiling people and rainbows. I was going to be one of them. I was going to be a proud, honest, open lesbian. In Toronto at least. When I moved to Toronto, I threw myself into the queer world, saturated myself. I went to all the events, joined all of the clubs. I found fast, if not lasting, friendships.

I took a deep breath and I started coming out. The first person I ever came out to was a girl I don't know anymore. A girl who sat down next to me during frosh week and asked if I had a boyfriend. For the first time in my life I didn't lie or give a half-answer. "No ... I don't have a boyfriend. Actually, I'm gay." I wore rainbows and told everybody I met. I was compensating for too many years of silence. I wasn't going to tell my family, though. I couldn't. Then my younger sister called me from home. Laura had been saying for years, "Just come out!" She wasn't joking, she wasn't teasing and she wasn't putting me down. She was just trying to get me to express the truth she had known for years. So she tried again: "I know you're gay." I was shaking, but could only answer, "I'm not." "Come on, just admit it. I don't care. Just admit it. You're gay. Just admit it." I was terrified. I was frustrated. I was tired. "Fine, you know what? I am. Are you happy now?" Her tone never changed: "Yes, very. So, when are you going to tell the parents?" I tried to avoid the question. I tried to deny the possibility. I knew I had to, though. So I decided I would the next time I called home.

My mother called. The conversation was about bus tickets, the minor details of an upcoming visit. I remember all the details so clearly. My white phone, the fake wood furniture, the blue rug where I curled up and choked out, "I'm gay." Lesbian was too big a word, had too many syllables. I could barely get the words out. I cried, but she didn't. At least not then. I sobbed. She told me that it was all right, that she didn't care, that she had never thought about it; but she wondered why I hadn't told her sooner. She asked me whether I would tell my father or whether she should. I said she should. I still don't know the details of that conversation. When my father next spoke to me, he was awkward, quieter than he usually is. It was sad; it was strange. Even though he said it was okay, in many ways I felt like a stranger.

After telling my parents, I started telling my friends. My best friend and I had known each other since kindergarten, but I had been lying to her for years, telling her stories of made up crushes and feigned interest. I told her the truth in an e-mail. She called me that night to say it was okay, but okay doesn't always mean okay. Later she would ask if I had ever had a crush on her, and even though I said no, I didn't hear from her again for three months. I wish I could see what would have happened if I hadn't told her, if things were different. Maybe we would still be close; maybe we grew apart for different reasons. All I know is that we rarely speak even now, three years later. Maybe we started to grow apart earlier, though. Maybe it happened the day she first told me about a crush on a boy, and I knew we just weren't coming from the same place anymore. I don't know.

Even when I did come out, even when I did face my fears and put on a proud face, my shame wasn't gone. I still thought my identity was wrong, a perversion. I still cried a lot. I still cut sometimes. This was supposed to be my perfect world, my freedom ... but it wasn't. Everything that my classmates had called wrong, everything my teachers had silenced ... it was me. I remember the first time I saw two boys kiss, as they walked me home from one of the various meetings I had started attending. My stomach turned; I blushed and looked away. I was ashamed for them. I was ashamed for myself. Somewhere I still believed that this was all wrong. Even through that, though, I knew I couldn't lie anymore.

It is difficult to explain exactly the effect T.E.A.C.H. has had on me. The training opened my mind to ideas and information that hadn't been a part of the first eighteen years of my life. Actually beginning to facilitate workshops and answer people's questions not only gave me the opportunity to challenge their homophobia, it gave me a chance to challenge my own. In questioning their presumptions, I questioned my own. I slowly began to accept and then celebrate who I was. This process was long, and it isn't over yet. Maybe it will never be. There are always more presumptions and assumptions to face.

Coming out has given me a very different understanding of homophobia. I had experienced it, mostly in an indirect way, throughout my life. In the whispered rumors, the locker-room insecurity, the casual insults of my education. In the silence that surrounded the entire subject. I had learned how to remain invisible, though, to deflect it so I wouldn't become a target. Coming out ended that process for me. I have experienced homophobia differently since then — in insults, in avoidance, in violence. And this is how I know I've changed, become stronger. I refuse to lower my head or to blend into other people's expectations. I refuse to apologize for my honesty, my identity or my pride. Coming out gave me the security to step outside my narrow definitions and borders, to question how I identify myself and whether my identifications are honest. My identity has in many ways shifted, in many ways it is perpetually shifting. I identify proudly as queer — one of the words I used to be the most frightened of hearing. I celebrate the intersections of my identity and my own individuality. I look back at things I've lost or missed. I look back at the moments I've spent feeling very sad, scared or alone.

There is a lot I wish hadn't happened and that I know is still happening to thousands of people. There are no true stories with completely happy endings, so I can offer only this: If you asked me now whether I would change if I could, I wouldn't. I wouldn't give up my education, my love or my pride for anything.

This Is Not a Coming Out Story

Emmy Pantin

I joined T.E.A.C.H. *in the fall of 1995. I learned so much from T.E.A.C.H. and made lots of friends. It was challenging to do anti-homophobia workshops in high schools and I learned a lot. Now if I'm ever confronted with a difficult presentation or situation, I think to myself:* that's nothing!

When I was thirteen, my best friend moved to a small town in southern Ontario. We had been inseparable up to that point, having witnessed each other's most difficult moments growing up together. I didn't know how I would survive without her. Our parents agreed to let me visit her for extended periods of time, even letting me go to school with her for weeks at a time in the fall and winter.

My best friend lived in an old schoolhouse in the countryside, with the original blackboards on the walls, although all the desks had been removed. Her bedroom was the old cloakroom. There was a bunk bed to accommodate me, but we usually slept together in the bottom bed.

Shortly after having moved to the country, my friend discovered the Friday night teen dances at the Legion Hall in the closest small town.

We would catch a ride into town, usually with a neighbor, and hang out, slow dancing to cheesy late-'80s music.

One day, a boy asked me for a dance. I looked nervously at my best friend. Her discomfort was palpable. I did not want to dance, but I knew it would have shamed her greatly if I did not. She needed me to dance with him to affirm my heterosexuality, and thereby hers, to everyone in the small community she lived in. The boy, in his Maple Leafs hockey sweater, grabbed my hand and pulled me onto the dance floor for the final song of the night. The last song, as always, was "Stairway to Heaven": the longest song in the history of music. I was mortified as we shuffled back and forth, and he drummed along to the song on my back. I realized I just wanted to be with my best friend, but that I had to dance with this boy to protect her reputation in this small town.

Is this my coming out story?

Queer is not a visible marker: One must articulate it. The coming out story is integral to creating a queer identity. T.E.A.C.H. workshops always include personal stories. Every queer kid has his or her coming out story.

T.E.A.C.H. helped me to literally shape my own story, my identity.

When I was fourteen, the distance from my friend in the country became unbearable. We barely spoke anymore. She became engrossed in the drama of the friends she made there, and I made a new best friend.

My new best friend and I also used to sleep in a single bed. We squeezed into bed together as our hips were growing. At night we would kiss and whisper to each other promises of love and belonging.

One day she said, "I don't think I like boys."

"Yeah, me neither," I said.

Is this my coming out story?

The year I turned seventeen, I was working part-time doing workshops about healthy sexuality for teenagers. We handed out condoms at concerts and other events. I received extensive training about STDs, HIV and AIDS, reproduction and anti-racism. I made some lifelong friends; I got to go to all kinds of concerts and events. My boss was amazing and fun, as were my coworkers. It was a teenage dream job.

A few months after I started as a sexual health peer educator, my coworker and I were called to do an HIV and AIDS workshop at a youth center. The youth knew all the myths about AIDS and none of the facts. We struggled throughout the workshop. The group of about ten teenagers yelled at us about faggots and dykes and how they all had AIDS. Neither of us had any idea what to say. We didn't know how to respond. The only ammunition I had was, "That's not true." I came home that night weeping, feeling like a lamb thrown to wolves. The next day I told my boss that I would refuse to do another AIDS workshop without first having had anti-homophobia training. Anti-homophobia training to an AIDS educator is safety training. My boss arranged for T.E.A.C.H. to do a workshop for us.

During the workshop, I listened really closely. I wanted to get whatever information I could. But the thing I remember the most is their stories. A whole bunch of things contributed to my coming out, but the part that gave me room and permission to claim the identity of lesbian was the way one of the T.E.A.C.H. panelists described herself in her story at that workshop. Up to that point there wasn't much that I identified with at Church and Wellesley. I went to high school about a block away from the infamous corner, but could never see myself hanging out there. I was more a Queen West sort of teenager. The T.E.A.C.H. panel was made up of people who were all different from each other; this made me think there was room for me to be different too.

At the end of the workshop I raised my hand and asked, "How did you know you were gay?" The responses didn't satisfy me. I asked again and again. I finally realized very quietly and privately what I had wanted to ask instead: "Can you tell me if I'm gay?" The following year I became a member of T.E.A.C.H.

Is this my coming out story?

When I was working as a sexual health peer educator, I first became comfortable with sexuality in general, then my own sexuality more specifically. While I was in T.E.A.C.H., Lynne

Fernie made a film about it called *School's Out*. In the video, Jane Rule makes a comment about the connection between homophobia and sex-phobia:

> Where does the homophobia come from? I think it comes at the extreme end of a society that is anti-sexual. My sense is that heterosexuals have been taught to be decently ashamed of their own sexuality, and then here come these people who are saying, "We're proud to be homosexual." Now, if they're decently ashamed, certainly we should be at least as decently ashamed as they are. And if we're not, we really are shocking to them. And I've always wanted to organize heterosexual pride day so we could T.E.A.C.H. them to be okay about their sexuality and then I think they would give us less of a bad time.

Shame silences stories; pride encourages us to tell them over and over again.

I'm not sure if I can remember the exact story I used to tell during the panel part of the T.E.A.C.H. workshops. I didn't know I'd forgotten my coming out story until recently, when at a ten-year reunion of T.E.A.C.H., I saw some of the crew who were in T.E.A.C.H. at the same time I was. They seemed to remember my coming out story better than I did.

After a while it got boring to tell the same stories over and over again. Sometimes it would seem as though it wasn't even true anymore, anyway. The words would be true, the details would be true, but the story itself was not really the story you wanted to tell. Sometimes we weren't in the mood or were feeling particularly vulnerable, so we'd tell a different story. Narratives would shift as our identities and moods would shift.

At the end of a T.E.A.C.H. workshop, people would ask us questions. We would give the participants the opportunity to write their questions anonymously. Some would see this as an opportunity to come out or clarify things in order to get an idea about how they might identify, just as I did when I attended that first T.E.A.C.H. workshop. Other kids saw it as an opportunity to write down insults and homophobic attacks. We were glad to edit those out or respond to them directly, depending on our feelings of vulnerability and level of ability.

And then there were the sex questions: "How do two men do it?" Sometimes it seemed like the whole time we were speaking, the participants were picturing us "doing it." Whenever I was asked that question, I would answer, "Use your imagination." For many high-school kids, sex exists in the realm of imagination. Before kids came to a T.E.A.C.H. workshop, sexuality may have seemed limited to a heterosexual humping activity. After a T.E.A.C.H. workshop, the limits of what was possible opened up. Suddenly, all kinds of relationships became possible, ones never considered before, sexual as well as platonic.

Our stories are populated with all kinds of people: parents, friends and lovers. T.E.A.C.H. is about conceiving of all the possibilities and creating new relationships — between individual facilitators, between facilitators and workshop participants, and between workshop participants and other queers who aren't even in the room.

In my first year of university, I tried to get involved with the student lesbian and gay collective. My friend, a lovely gay man, and I sauntered over to the first meeting of the year. It was early fall and the air was electric with possibility.

The meeting was boring and long. Across the room from me, a young woman was stretched out across the back of a sofa, staring at me intensely. She introduced herself later that evening and invited me for tea at her house. A few hours later, I was sitting in the kitchen of a massive colonial house filled to the brim with students, organic food and chai masala. After an evening of talk and laughter, she offered to walk me home. As we walked down the street, I suddenly stopped. I grabbed her sweater and pulled her behind a tree. We stayed there, in the cool fall night, kissing for hours.

Is this my coming out story?

When was the exact moment I came out? Was it the time I danced with that boy at the teen dance despite my longing to be with that girl across the room? or the time I told my best friend I didn't like boys? Or was it later? the first time I kissed a girl?

I come out every day. My coming out story grows and expands with my life....

Coming Out in the 905

Anthony Collins

One of the great pleasures *of working with other youth in a community of dedicated anti-homophobia peer educators has been hearing the coming out stories. We repeat them so many times, we often joke that we could tell each other's stories as easily as our own. When speaking to groups about homophobia, sharing bits and pieces of autobiography can be a very effective strategy to grab the audience's attention. On the relatively rare occasions when I am speaking in front of a group that is inattentive or disrespectful, I usually find that as soon as I begin relating my own experiences, the mood in the room changes. Telling our stories is recognized as a difficult and solemn act (though most of our narratives also have humorous moments) — one that deserves close attention. Our stories are also teaching tools based on our experiences, which we can bend and shape, shorten or draw out to fill the space of any classroom and to highlight certain messages. Often we have only a few minutes each to tell a group about our coming out experiences. So we learn to use our stories strategically.*

The story I am presenting here is a longer, more detailed rendering of a narrative I have repeated to hundreds of people in classrooms and community spaces in Toronto since 2001. When I began facilitating workshops for T.E.A.C.H. and for SpeakOut, a similar program within the Toronto District School Board, I was nineteen. Since then, I have visited elementary, middle and high schools throughout the city and have also spoken to groups of teachers, administrators, student leaders and social workers.

Before beginning this story, I want to acknowledge my colleagues in SpeakOut and T.E.A.C.H., as well as the students who have participated in our workshops. I have learned so much from the comments and questions we receive, and my views have evolved thanks to the wisdom and experience of other talented volunteers. Most importantly, I wish to thank the coordinators of SpeakOut and T.E.A.C.H. for their constant support, mentorship and inspiration.

I grew up in Thornhill, a fairly wealthy suburb of Toronto that forms part of the "905 Belt" (so named because of its area code) surrounding the city. Suburban norms and expectations meant that my decision not to obtain a driver's license provoked incomprehension and near outrage on the part of some of my family members. Growing up in this bubble, I had the warped perception that because my friends' families often seemed to have more disposable income than mine, I wasn't well off. I later realized that most of us were steeped in class privilege. Families with fewer than four bedrooms in their homes or fewer than two cars were rare. Although there was a large Jewish population and a significant degree of racial diversity, many kinds of difference were superficially flattened out and glossed over with a veneer of shared class privilege and the language of liberal multiculturalism. Though I would not have believed so while growing up, there was a good deal of racism and anti-Semitism in the area.

I fit into my community in many ways: I was white, middle class and Jewish. Still, from an early age I felt excluded in other respects. I was never interested in sports and had a terrible fear of gym class and of competing athletically in the schoolyard. I often found it difficult to relate to friends my own age. And I remember being teased often — not viciously, but enough to cause me a great deal of anguish. I was teased for being a brainer, for being a teacher's pet, for having wild, curly hair. On several occasions I was mistaken for a girl.

In retrospect, I see the early signs of queerness in my young self. I idolized handsome actors and musicians, going through various crushes and later rationalizing that I didn't *want* these men but wanted to be *like* them. I don't recall consciously considering my own sexuality until about grade eight, which is when I developed a very tight friendship with M.M. We grew so close that he would phone me at the same time every day after school. He used to tell me about crushes and fantasies he had, about girls he would like to date. I didn't have the same fantasies that he did, but spending time with him was exciting and fulfilling for me. I had such a strong desire to be with him that I would walk over to his house almost every day, hoping he might be outside playing basketball on the driveway. I felt protective of him and jealous when he spent time with our other friends. When others alluded to the closeness of our friendship, it made me swell with pride. I didn't realize at the time that I had a crush on him, but his respect and approval of me as a friend and equal meant everything to me. So in order to have something to offer in exchange for the secrets he shared, and not knowing what sexual and romantic attraction was supposed to feel like, I would lie and make up stories about being attracted to girls at school.

We entered grade nine at a large high school, where my social circle quickly grew. I finally started to meet people I had much more in common with, people who would become my closest friends. One of them was Audrey. She and I hit it off right away. We had similar interests and loved to chat with each other about our favorite books and films. We also had a similar sense of humor. I found myself thinking of her and wanting to spend time with her. I figured that this was as close as I would come to the feelings of attraction that my male friends had for the girls they liked. So I flirted with Audrey and we started dating. We were together for six months during grade ten. In the middle of this relationship, I began to realize that my feelings for her were more those of friendship than of sexual or romantic attraction. I also started to have the inkling that my feelings for M.M. and for other boys might mean that my sexuality was somehow different. I had never met any out queer people — no relatives, teachers, friends or acquaintances — so I had to search discreetly for role models.

I looked first to media for information. I read anything I could get my hands on that dealt with LGBTQ people or issues. I rented queer movies. This was before *Will & Grace* and *Queer As Folk*, so Ellen DeGeneres's coming out was about the extent of a queer presence on TV. I hoarded magazines and surreptitiously clipped and filed away queer-related articles from the *Toronto Star*. I sought out alternative publications like *Xtra!* I was lucky in that most of the media representations of queerness that I consumed made it easy for me to imagine myself in the life. I saw myself reflected in the predominant images of white, middle-class gay men.

I also learned by exploring the city. I had always looked forward to family trips into downtown Toronto. When I was in high school, the city became the place I escaped to after school and on weekends. Audrey and I used to walk around the city together, taking architectural tours and going to bookstores, cinemas and cafés. The times I went downtown by myself were the times I explored the queer side of the city. I walked nervously up and down Church Street, ducked into the 519 Community Centre, saw queer-themed films at the Carlton and stood at the back of the crowd one year to watch the Pride Parade. Traveling downtown from Thornhill, I remember feeling fleetingly connected to a larger world of urban histories, relationships and possibilities. Toronto's rich cultures, streetscapes and public spaces all contributed to the feeling of vitality I had when I was downtown. These forays filled a void in me left by Thornhill's flat, suburban landscape, which offered no clues about queer culture or about to how to lead a life that didn't include cookie-cutter homes, meandering semi-private streets and mall culture. I was lucky that my middle-class privilege allowed me the leisure to fill the gaps in my education.

As I learned more and found role models, a swirling mass of thoughts and emotions began to resolve into a coherent expression of identity. If others were living their lives with openness and integrity, then perhaps I, too, could feel pride in being different. I tentatively attached a new label to myself — gay — and secretly wore it around for a while. It seemed to suit me. It made me unique, and I felt all the more mature for having overcome homophobia and heterosexism in coming out to myself. At the same time, I felt dishonest and shameful of my ongoing relationship with Audrey. I broke up with her at the end of that summer. I didn't tell her the truth but gave the excuse that I wasn't ready for the responsibility of a relationship.

It wasn't until about six months later that my pride in my gay identity and an eagerness to share my desires and frustrations prompted me to come out. I chose Audrey as the first person to tell. She was still my closest friend, and I knew that at the very least, I could trust her not to reveal my secret. The guilt I felt for not having told her the truth, as well as the exciting prospect of making my declaration, wouldn't let me wait any longer. I wrote a coming out speech, rehearsed it, and delivered it slowly and nervously to her one night. We were in a mall after the stores had closed, and there were few people around. "I couldn't wait any longer to tell you this," I started off. "I don't want to hurt you, but you have to know." Here I took a deep breath. "When we broke up, I swear all the things I told you were true. *Really.* But I didn't give you the real reason. There's no easy way to say this ... I'm gay."

They were the hardest words I had ever forced out. My heart was pounding. At first Audrey thought I was joking, but when it sank in, we both became quite emotional. She had lots of questions, but almost instantly, in a show of great maturity, she became my supporter. To lighten the mood, she said, "This is just like that stupid Jennifer Aniston movie!" (We had seen a preview for *The Object of My Affection* a couple of weeks earlier.) We talked for a few hours that evening and even started comparing notes on boys that we thought were cute. "It's so weird to be talking to you about this," Audrey said that night as we discussed our favorite studs on *The Young and the Restless*. It was strange for me, too, to share these feelings for the first time. But from that point on, my rapport with Audrey felt more natural than it ever had. I will always be in awe of the strong and elegant way in which she handled the news of my coming out, quickly working through her initial shock and feeling of betrayal to reassure me and shift our friendship. She understood so much. I took great strength from her support and from the secret bond that only we shared at the time. We whispered back and forth in class and continued to escape downtown after school together to further our worldly education. *The Object of My Affection* became the first gay-themed movie we saw together.

My relationship with Audrey later gave me the confidence to come out selectively to more friends. I even told M.M. that I was gay, although by that time we had grown apart. The reactions I received were mostly positive. When I was seventeen, I decided to come out to my parents, which remains the most difficult thing I've ever had to do. I told my mother first, and let her relay the news to my dad. My parents and I are very close, and my mom had sensed that I was keeping something from her for quite some time. But she was in no way prepared for what I had to say. She was shocked and went through several stages of understanding and accepting my news. At first, she was sure that I was wrong, or that I was going through a phase that would pass. When she realized I was certain, she wondered if she was to blame for my turning out this way. My father had lots of rational objections. He told me that same-sex attraction was an experience common to most boys, that my feelings might change later on. One of the things my parents and I argued about was my intention to come out to other people. I had visions of raising hell as a gay high-school activist, but for a long time my parents were very uncomfortable with the thought of my coming out to anyone else, because they didn't want people to judge me and doors to be closed to me because of my sexual orientation.

It was a challenge to have to defend my new identity so firmly to my parents in those emotionally charged discussions, but the experience gave me some of the tools that I still use to make sense of myself and to explain my sexuality to others. My mom and dad had always been extremely liberal with my sister and me. The trust that let me broach the subject of my sexuality with them was reaffirmed. It took them a while to get used to the idea of having a gay son — at first they were as limited by the confining expectations of heterosexism as I had been. For a few months we didn't discuss it much, but when we started talking again after that silence, they had come to a much deeper understanding. Since then, I have felt comfortable being completely open about my life and about sharing my thoughts and values with them.

Later in grade twelve, I met Jason, my first gay friend at school. We came out to each other during one of our frequent downtown trips: In a busy bookstore, I suggestively picked up a copy of *Out* magazine and waited until he came near enough to see what I was reading. He looked up at me, paused, then asked hesitantly if I was gay. I said yes and waited for his reaction. After only a beat, he responded, "Oh ... me too!" It was a response I had hardly dared to hope for. We eagerly made plans to get together and share our stories. We pined after crushes together and railed against homophobes. We also dated briefly that year. Coming out to Jason let me explore a new range of experiences and dialogues. We tested our identities and ideas, learning from one another. We were, for the most part, not out to others at school, but spent time together and communicated in furtive remarks and glances. As with Audrey, I felt a quiet pride and pleasure in our secret affinity, although our inhibition was frustrating at times.

Audrey and Jason both helped when, in my last year of high school, I co-founded and led a Rainbow Alliance. Our group was modeled after the gay-straight alliances that we had heard were starting up in schools elsewhere in Canada and the United States. In the first several months, we held weekly meetings and organized our school's first Pride Week, which included anti-homophobia workshops, a film festival, a visual display and presentations to staff and students. I was able to lead these activities without being completely out, since the premise of our group was that it incorporated straight allies as well as LGBTQ people. However, when I entered the University of Toronto that fall, I resolved to be completely out to everyone I met. Since then, my sexual and political identities have increasingly informed the direction of my studies as well as my career path.

Once I began to move in university-based social circles and

devote myself further to activism, my political views underwent a profound change, and I shed my narrow gay identity for a broader, queerer outlook. My high-school anti-homophobia work began to seem quaint in comparison. Looking back now, I am struck by how much my involvement in the Rainbow Alliance was guided by my own coming out process. I was still at a naïve stage in my activism that could be summed up as "I'm here, I'm queer!" and did not look beyond the heterosexism I experienced to interrogate other forms of privilege from which I benefited. My high-school anti-homophobia work largely reflected my own identity — for instance, most of the films I programmed in the Pride Week film festival represented white, middle-class gay men like myself. Similarly, the anti-homophobia discourse I employed at the time was ignorant of the very different lived experiences of lesbian, bisexual and trans youth, and of the realities for youth who are marginalized on the basis of race, class, ability, etc., in addition to sexual orientation and/or gender identity.

I commuted downtown daily during my first and second years of university, but grew tired and depressed having to trudge back to the suburbs every night. I found the lack of queer culture and nightlife in Thornhill stifling. I went through a low period in second year and ended up moving downtown. As a result, I was able to meet more friends, have more opportunities for dating, and devote myself more fully to equity-related studies, employment and volunteering. I now spend most of my time in spaces where being queer is at least a non-issue and usually an asset. I have to remind myself that most others don't have the network of encouragement and support that I do. But though my sexual identity receives a lot of affirmation, I still have the opportunity to challenge myself and the limits of my thoughts and beliefs often.

As my co-facilitators in T.E.A.C.H. are fond of reminding students, coming out is a process that never ends. There are always new situations that demand that we disrupt heterosexist expectations by speaking out and taking up space as queers. The way we come out and the language we use, however, can change over time. I now identify as queer in most activist and academic spaces. The difference between gay and queer, for me, is more a political nuance than a reflection on my sexual attraction. Gay carries more baggage than queer, its stereotypes and associations are more fixed and rigid. While the word queer recalls painful histories of subjugation, it also connotes a powerful readiness to reclaim those histories in the process of demanding radical change. Queer is usually considered more representative and embracing of the diversity within the LGBTQ community than gay. I still shift back and forth between the two labels with little dissonance, sometimes wishing to connect myself with a proud history of gay activism, and sometimes preferring to align myself with a more inclusive and differently politicized community of queer youth. I am lucky that, as a man who's attracted to men, my sexual and gender identity have always been relatively uncomplicated. The word "gay" — often the simplest word at hand for closeted youth because of its wide currency — never seemed to suit me too badly. In the past, when I've used it to come out to friends and family, "gay" has felt right to me and made sense to the listener.

In this version of my story, I have the luxury of calling myself queer and using the word as a shorthand symbol for "lesbian, gay and bisexual," whereas in classrooms, we don't always have the chance to explain the politics of the word "queer" and to distinguish our take on it from the way it is still hurled as an insult in schools. Explaining the proper use of the terms "lesbian," "gay," "bisexual," "transgender" and "transsexual," as well as debunking stereotypes associated with them, is usually the first step we are able to undertake toward challenging homophobia given the limited time available to us. We are forced to make other deletions that feel unnatural: For instance, we cannot make any explicit mention of sex in the classroom. We have to separate our work from sex education in order to preserve our mandate to do anti-discrimination work in a time of continuing conservative backlash. But so much of coming out as lesbian, gay or bisexual — or, for that matter, of being heterosexual — *is* about sex and our desires and feelings surrounding it.

In trying to write the story of my coming out that I have recited so many times, I have come to realize how much storytelling has become a performance or ritual for me, albeit one with many variations. While it makes for an effective performance, narrating this journey can sometimes seem too rehearsed, too remote from my visceral memories of coming out to myself and to others. I was nervous about committing this story to paper because I thought it would be forever reified in these precise terms. But this is just one version. Much of coming out is about coming into language — identifying ourselves with words and ideas, and choosing which words we will use to make ourselves coherent and legible to others. Our stories — and sometimes our memories — are therefore shifting and malleable. We trim and amend them in order to turn messy life experience into a meaningful narrative of becoming, but the beginnings and endings are never fixed. And like all other versions, this retelling of my coming out is incomplete. The story was heavily edited long before it reached this volume, even before I said the words in a classroom for the first time. Deletions and substitutions have been made for the sake of brevity, to expedite important messages and to protect myself from reliving certain emotions. In the future, I'm sure the language and means of communication I use to tell my story will change again many times. But the memory of struggling across language to put my desires and identity into words for the first time will remain with me.

At a Messy Intersection

ayden isak hoffman-scheim

This is my story. *This is the story that I tell at T.E.A.C.H. workshops. I find it really healing to share it with people. I also feel privileged to be able to share my story. Because queer and trans youth are very often silenced, I can't wait for a time when all queer and trans youth will have the same opportunity as I have now. We all need a space to tell our stories, to be heard. So for me being able to tell this story is an important act of resistance. I tell my story often and loudly. I tell it to break the silence, to educate, to inspire. I tell my story in the hope that someone who hears me might think about the revolutionary potential of simply loving themselves and sharing their stories.*

I remember the night I started to come out to my mother. I was fourteen. It was a windy Friday night in October. It was so windy that sitting under the window in the living room, I could hardly hear myself talk. That made coming out even harder. I was scared of saying the wrong thing. After mumbling for half an hour, I finally choked out, "I'm bisexual." A week later I corrected myself, or so I thought. I told her that I was, in fact, a lesbian.

I was raised in a religious Jewish home. My father was a Conservative rabbi. My mother was a social worker. I kept kosher, went to synagogue every week and spoke Hebrew. I went to an Orthodox private Jewish day school. Everyone I knew there was white, rich and Jewish. This upbringing sheltered and isolated me from the world around me.

But I always felt different and I was made to feel different at the school by the girls in my class. They would never let me forget that I was fat, smart, a budding feminist or just plain weird. They constantly made fun of, excluded and attacked me. This made me angry and depressed. In addition to this I was also dealing with family problems. My mother had always struggled with a severe eating disorder and other mental health issues. During that time her mental and physical health was deteriorating. Things at home were very tense and the tension seemed to keep growing. When I was twelve, I could no longer handle the anger and depression I felt for how I was being treated at school or the sadness and confusion I felt in relation to my mother. I ended up in a youth mental health ward, and then I went to live in a group home for two years. Living there was horrible and I was mistreated. However, this experience helped me learn so much about myself. I learned how to be resilient and strong, and how to resist adversity. I learned to name my experiences. I learned that I was being abused by the mental health system, and that it wasn't just uncomfortable for me — it was wrong. I learned to stand up for myself, something I had never done before.

If one good thing came out of all this, it was that I got out of the Jewish day school. That place had been a very negative space for me. While living at the group home I was enrolled in a public school. I met kids from all kinds of different backgrounds; I was exposed to diversity in terms of race, religion and class. I learned a lot and thought about and saw many new things. All these made me feel less sheltered and isolated.

I was also exposed to sex and sexuality through my peers and the school's health classes. The messages I got about these issues were helpful and not so helpful. I visited some good websites and I was also exposed to porn. All this learning, thinking and being exposed to sexual things made me realize that I was sexually different. At fourteen, the experience of being freshly exposed to the real world was intense, but I still needed to learn many more things. In addition to making all these discoveries, I was also dealing with moving back home after two years in group homes. It was a roller coaster–like few months.

I continued to learn. When I found out about lesbians, I identified with them, as they seemed to be the closest thing to myself. They liked girls and I knew I liked girls. They were masculine, as I was and wanted to be. So I decided to be a lesbian.

But it was not easy to do. I know now that on that windy October night I started the process of coming out not only to my mother but also to myself. Once I told my mother, things started to roll. She told my father but it took him many months to accept me as a lesbian.

My friends reacted very well to my coming out, and so I became very out at my school. Everything seemed fine until the school social worker called for a meeting with my family. She told my parents and me that I had been essentially recruiting other students and had made two boys become bisexual. I was told to "stop talking about the gay issue all the time." If I did not, I would have to leave the school. I wasn't going to put up with that kind of nonsense, so I left before they could tell me to leave. My parents were shocked, but tried to defend the school's position. I was less hurt than mystified by the whole experience.

While looking at alternative schools on the school board's website, I found the Triangle Program, an alternative school for lesbian, gay, bisexual and transgendered youth, and I decided to go there. At Triangle, I really felt comfortable and respected. During my first year there, I learned so much about queer history and community — my history, my community. I became involved with various queer youth groups and joined T.E.A.C.H. I had become an activist. In my second year at Triangle, I had some inward experiences. I started to be exposed to all the options one has as a queer person. I learned from some of my peers that sexual orientation and gender were not concepts as rigid as I had once thought. This came at a time when I had already been questioning myself as a lesbian. I had thoughts and feelings that being one just wasn't right for me. I was experiencing a nagging crush on my male friend's roommate, and I had an intense urge for the cashier at the health food store to call me "sir." I was searching for something new.

However, I had to put these thoughts and feelings on hold. Because of my activism, I was asked to be a part of a documentary film about students in the Triangle Program that would be shown on CBC and screened at film festivals all over North America. This and the fact that I had become known in the community as "the young Jewish lesbian activist" made my questioning process very difficult. The documentary was near completion and part of me felt that I had to stay a lesbian and that I had to put my feelings away.

But I soon realized that no matter how hard I tried, my feelings weren't going away. I was growing more uncomfortable in my body. I was cringing when people called me "she." I was sick of hiding my attractions to men. I was starting to see myself as a queer guy, but nobody else was. I knew I had to come out again and this was as difficult to do as it had been the first time. But I knew I had to. So I started to come out as trans a few months before turning sixteen. The first person I came out to was my best friend, who is trans himself. He was very supportive and so were my closest friends, whom I told as well.

I also had to come out to my family. This time, however, coming out to my parents as a queer boy was actually quite easy. Their reaction was muted. This wasn't because they accepted me as trans, but because their coping strategy was to simply ignore my second coming out. They still call me by my old name and refer to me as a lesbian; but aside from not recognizing or respecting my identity, they do support me in every other way, so I'm much luckier than many transpeople. There are still people in my family and former communities who call me by my old name or don't know me anymore. I am coming out to all of them, but slowly. Some people don't understand, while others surprise me with positive reactions. Coming out is an ongoing process.

Since I had built a home for myself in the queer community, I thought that it would be easier to come out there. But to my surprise and disappointment, one of the hardest parts about coming out as trans was realizing that some people in the community weren't as accepting as I had thought they would be. I realized that many gays and lesbians I had considered friends were very transphobic. I think that this realization was, in the end, a blessing. I got to see who my true friends and allies were, and through this process I also became aware of how other oppressions are at work within the queer community. My experience opened my eyes to the racism, classism, sexism and other forms of discrimination present in the queer community. I also learned that as a white middle-class person, I have privileges. So I learned how to recognize that and challenge myself. I also learned how to work in the anti-oppression struggle and to become an ally. Today, I am as involved in the community as Ayden "Andy" Scheim, a proud queer FTM (female-to-male).

Nonetheless, the most important thing I've learned is to love and embrace all of who I am. It's impossible to create social change without first changing the way you feel about yourself. When I first came out, my reaction to homophobia was to be queer first and foremost. Now I see my experiences as a Jew, a survivor of the mental health system, a proud fat person, a trans person and a youth as being as integral to who I am. I am also not the manliest guy in the world. I'm a sissy (I use the term "genderqueer") and I love that part of myself; I don't feel that I should try to hide it. I am the sum of all my parts. All these parts have their own stories and all meet somewhere, at a messy intersection, since things like identity are never clearly cut-and-dried. Having said all this, I refuse to have my being cut up and put into boxes.

I remember that windy October night when I started to come out to my mother. I'm amazed at how far I've come in the three years since then.

Alone

Andrew Standell Mills

I used to not be able to tell my story without tears, but now that I have dealt with the emotion and the trauma, I can finally tell it. I am actually thankful for what happened, as it has helped me learn more about myself. After all, strength is not measured by never falling, but in rising each time we fall. I believe that, and I try to focus on the good things. This story was written before I joined T.E.A.C.H., but the first time I shared it with people was at a T.E.A.C.H. workshop. After telling it at a couple of T.E.A.C.H. workshops, I found it was too long, so now I tell another one instead. But I decided to share this story now because I know that many people have been through similar things. The Internet is becoming an important part of everybody's lives and certainly can be invaluable for queer youth who feel they have no other place to turn. But it also can be a dangerous place. This story is really about a first love gone wrong, and I think almost everybody can relate to that on some level. So let me start by asking you a question:

Have you ever felt alone?

Really, truly alone?

As though the universe is leaving you behind and everybody in the world is taking part in lives that all somehow leave you out?

No matter what effort you make to join in, take part and connect with people, all your efforts fail.

Some efforts get further than others, but in the end, they all fail.

In the end, everybody leaves you.

In the end, you're all alone.

Even the people closest to you are so far away.

Even the people who know the most about you know nothing at all.

Even the people you trust the most will betray you in the end.

You're in an invisible realm that nobody can penetrate and that you can't get rid of.

It's lonely in there, and there's only so much air.

Sooner or later, the air is going to run out and you're going to fade away into nothingness.

Only then will people notice.

Only then will they pause to reflect.

But only for a moment.

Life will continue as normal, and soon even the memory of you will be no more.

Have you ever really felt alone?

I have....

That's how I felt in the summer after grade eleven. I was sixteen and in the weeks leading up to the start of grade twelve, feeling alone and with no particular desire to live, I ran away from home. I grew up in British Columbia, so I took off to my favorite place in the whole world: the mountains. I spent five nights by myself in the Garibaldi Mountain Range, most of them trying to figure out the events of the past year and where exactly I went wrong. A lot happened that year, but I'll go back to just before the start of the summer.

I had been browsing the Internet for a long time by now, searching mostly for pictures of cute boys. It took me many years to figure out that it was more than a curiosity that I had with boys, that it was in fact an attraction in every sense of the word. One day I was looking at the links section of a Yahoo! Group, and I saw advertised a support group for gay, bi, and questioning boys aged eighteen and under. It was nothing special or official, just a club started by another young guy. I applied to join and was accepted.

Reading the posted messages by the members, I suddenly realized that I was not the only guy in the world going through this weird thing called coming out! It was totally and completely amazing. There were guys of all ages from around the world in there, sharing their stories and their lives. Some of them even had boyfriends! Even though it seemed at first as though I was on the outside looking into a tightly knit group, I soon found out how accepting and welcoming they were. When I came out to my mom in May, which didn't go over so well at first, I immediately had tons of e-mails of support and friendship from people I didn't even know. That's when the power of support and friendship over the

Net first really struck me. Unfortunately, it wasn't long after that the dark side of the Net showed itself as well.

In early July, a new guy joined the group and posted a message giving a bit of info about himself. I checked out his profile and he had some cute pictures. It seemed, from reading his e-mail, that he felt the same way I did in a lot of ways. I wrote to him and told him that he didn't need to feel alone because there were others like him out there, and just because he didn't know any in real life didn't mean they weren't there. I basically introduced myself as well and said that I hoped to hear from him later. It was the first time ever I had e-mailed somebody from the group, and I had no idea how it was going to go. My heart just about leapt out of my body when he replied. I e-mailed him back right away, and so began an e-mail friendship. I would rush to my computer to see if he had written, and he told me that he did the same. Reading his e-mails was so cool because we had so much in common, and we were both connecting to another gay teen for the first time. After not much time at all, the word "love" was used. Gingerly at first, but then once we both said it we couldn't stop. I never would have thought it possible or believed it if it happened, but it truly was love at first ... write.

This continued for weeks, and each day we just fell deeper and deeper in love. Then one night I e-mailed him and it bounced back. I checked his profile and it wasn't there anymore. I tossed and turned that night, worried as to what might have happened. A million thoughts raced through my mind. In the morning I went immediately to my computer. There was an e-mail from a different account, and it showed up as a different name.

It was from him. He said (in short), "Andrew I'm sorry. I lied to you. That isn't my real name. I was too afraid of somebody finding me out. And those aren't my real pictures either. I am nowhere near that cute. I don't blame you if you never want to talk to me again."

I was in shock. The boy I trusted with my heart, my mind and my soul had lied to me. I went through the stages of grief and felt each one intensely. I didn't want to believe it was true. It was, and I was devastated. I wrote e-mails to him in tears, and he did the same. One day when I was really mad, I read old e-mails and picked out things that must have been lies. Like nicknames and stuff like that. I e-mailed him in a fury and let out all my anger. That night I went to a friend's house, but I couldn't get him off my mind. Over the course of the night, I slipped slowly into acceptance and figured that if all the pain and hurt I had been going through was what it took for us to be together, then it was worth it. I didn't care what he looked like. I didn't care what his name was. All I cared about was that his feelings were real, and so were mine.

I headed downstairs to use my friend's computer and logged into my mail to find his response to my angry e-mail. He said it was clear he had hurt me too much, and he couldn't even begin to tell me how sorry he was. He thanked me for being the light in his life, sharing my joy and love with him and other similar things. He said that we both knew it could never work out after what had happened, so we might as well end it now. He added a poem that meant a lot to the both of us and wrote "THE END...."

I e-mailed him in a panic, saying how sorry I was for getting mad, that it didn't matter anymore and that all I wanted to do was work it out. That e-mail got sent back due to yet another deleted account.

I went upstairs and walked out the door without saying a word. I was too numb to cry or feel anything. Two friends followed, as I was their ride home. It was probably the scariest ride home of their lives. I dropped off one friend, and when the second one asked me what was wrong, I burst into tears. I told him everything, bawling my eyes out. He told me not to fear, we would find the guy no matter what it took. We went back to my apartment and looked for clues from his old e-mails as to his true identity. He said that the name he had originally used was the one of a teacher he admired. We managed to track down that teacher in the city he lived in, and I got his phone number. My friend went home, and I managed to go to bed.

The next morning, I sat by my phone for three hours before I actually dialed this teacher in Indiana. I gave him a made-up story, because I didn't want to break the trust of the boy. I was hoping for some sort of clue. A last name or anything that would help me track him down. I simply couldn't live without him. The teacher wasn't much help, and I was pretty discouraged. Then, two hours later, I got an e-mail from him. He said that he tried to get out of my life and put me out of his, but he simply couldn't live without me. He wondered if I could ever forgive him and promised never to run away again. I wanted to make it work, and so we tried.

It was hard at first and very different too. But gradually things started to get better. Then one day he stopped e-mailing — not a word, not a warning, nothing. He just stopped. I didn't know what had happened, and for more than a month I remained in the dark. During the time I wrote that poem, I also ran away from home. I needed closure, and the lack of it had done crazy things to my emotions. The trip in the mountains really helped, and when I got back I felt a lot better. I thought I had dealt with everything and was ready to move on. I was wrong.

When I got back, I chatted a lot with a new guy who had joined the group. He seemed to have a lot of anger issues, so I started e-mailing him privately in an effort to help. Though I had shut myself off to getting close to anybody on the Net again, I was still able to make close friends with people. I grew to respect, like and above all trust this new guy — until I started to see similarities between him and the boy from the summer. Finally I confronted him about it, and he admitted to being the same guy. But before I could talk to him about it, he deleted his account and vanished yet again.

At that point, emotions came flooding back from the days before. Emotions I thought I had dealt with, but had just buried deep down. I felt abandoned. I felt betrayed. I felt things I had never felt before. More than anything, though, I felt alone. I wanted to go to bed and never wake up again. Without much thought, I took eight times the recommended dose of sleeping pills and attempted to commit suicide. Thankfully, I didn't take a high enough dosage to require medical attention. The truth is, I took all the ones I had but the bottle was almost out to begin with. Had there been more, I don't know how many others I would have taken or what the effect would have been.

As I lay in bed, I was paralyzed not only by the drugs but by fear as well. I came to understand the severity of what I had done, but I was unable to move or do anything to cry for help. My mind started swimming as I was slipping slowly into unconsciousness. I knew I had made a mistake, but I was also peculiarly happy at the same time. Soon, though, the happiness over the ease with which I was going unconscious began to scare me, and I tried to battle it. It was beyond my control, however, a product of my hasty actions. I came to the conclusion that all I could do was hope I would wake up in the morning and make a pledge to myself to get the help I needed and surely wanted. Then, darkness....

The next day was a haze for me. My mom went off to work without a clue; I just didn't wake up until the afternoon. When I finally did open my eyes, it was to a world seen through tunnel vision. My head was aching and the moment I sat up I became dizzy. I tried to stand and barely could. It took all the effort I could muster to walk and get dressed. The room was spinning and I felt as though I was the living dead. Every part of my body was still peacefully asleep. I could hardly force it to move. It seemed to take forever to make my way to the bus stop. It was as though every moment lasted forever and everything seemed in slow motion.

I knew where I was going, though. I got on the bus, went to school and went straight to my counselor. He was the head counselor at the school, somebody I respected and admired. He had helped me through some rough times over the years, and he already knew most of what was going on. We had spoken at great length after I returned from the mountains, but we both thought that the issue of the disappearing boy from the Internet was closed. My overdose was as much a surprise to him as it was to me. After I told him what happened, I asked him for help, and we arranged for me to meet with a suicide specialist.

I already felt that something within me had changed, however. I wasn't sure quite what it was at first, but undoubtedly the next few days went a long way toward making me the person I am today. That day I developed a mantra and kept saying it to myself: "I refuse to be a helpless victim to the whims and afflictions of others. I am who I am and I love myself. I am who I am and I accept myself. I am who I am and I am myself."

By the time I met with a suicide specialist, I had developed such a new outlook on life that she called me one of the most together young men she had ever met and said that I had made an amazing turnaround. I was not at risk, she decided, and I didn't need to meet with her again.

From that day on, I was better able to control the way I feel and how I act. I still am very emotional, but it's healthy emotion now, and *nobody* has the power to make me feel so low that ending it is the only option.

I received an e-mail some months later from the same guy. He said that it was finally time for a little truth from him. It turned out that the teacher I forced myself to call was, in fact, him. He is thirty-nine and he used a combination of real childhood events and his students' identities to pose as a sixteen-year-old. I cried, and I felt dirty and ashamed, but never even thought about suicide.

The reality is that the Internet can be an amazing thing for gay, bi or questioning teens. My online relationship opened doors I only dreamed existed and helped me to become more in tune with my sexuality. Really, I believe that there's no such thing as a mistake as long as you learn from it. To that end, I would not suggest that people not have online friends, and even online relationships. All I do suggest is that you be careful who you give your heart to. My Internet relationship felt like fate. Maybe it was.

Learning through stories i've told

j.t.s. berrigan

Putting these words on paper, *words i have spoken to hundreds of young people at T.E.A.C.H. workshops, made me realize that i was creating the opportunity for many more to know of my experiences. But it also reminded me of the limits of the written word. You will not know the tone this story has when i speak it or the speed at which words are said. You will be able to read what i have written but not have questions answered or areas expanded. Important information has also been left out, not because it has been forgotten, but because it may be too painful to retell. There are also places i left vague because they remain uncertain to me. So this story is only a piece of how i experienced coming out. Although i have come out to my family, i have never told them this story. This may be the impetus to do so.*

Let me tell you a story....

When folks explain how homophobia or heterosexism affected their lives, they often say, "Well i always felt different." My first experience of feeling different was through the color of my skin (brown) and my race (Black). i was born in Halifax, Nova Scotia, one of the most racially segregated cities i have ever seen. This is ironic because Nova Scotia is the province with the largest concentration of Black people in Canada. i was adopted into a wonderful family who cared for me and loved me. In my new family, my mother, my father and my sister, adopted a year and a half before i was, were all white. While growing up, i always heard stories about the Canadian east coast. These stories spoke of my family, but they did not include me as a Black person or, for that matter, the history of Black folks in Canada. The exception was the story of when my father first met a Black man on the railway when he was eighteen. So difference was never something new to me. i saw this difference at every family dinner and in every family picture. When i walked into a room, it was often the first thing people saw. When we moved to a suburban paradise in Ontario, the first comment from our neighbor's son about us was, "The new family moved in and there's a brown kid."

In this new place, i grew up with other middle-class children playing middle-class games. i was twelve when i first encountered a family who couldn't afford the expensive things my parents had given my sister and me throughout our lives. At the same time, i was the only Black child in a school of five hundred and remember many times being asked why my skin was brown and not having an answer. People tell me that these are innocent questions. They never seemed innocent to me. My social class and, no question, my parents' education often meant that i was included. But sooner rather than later i found out about a different kind of exclusion.

One of the first questions people ask folks who are lesbian, gay, bisexual, trans or queer is, "When did you know?" i can honestly say that when i was three years old i knew i was emotionally and physically attracted to men. But on a Monday afternoon when i was eleven, i was watching a TV show and i heard the words gay and lesbian used in a positive way for the first time. These words reflected more than any emotional or physical attractions i had had for men. This was the first time i knew i was sexually attracted to them in a way that my male friends were not.

But i had to learn how to know to say nothing about those feelings. In my family, my community, my faith we did not talk about those kinds of things. My elementary school teachers did not even mention the so-called evils of a man loving another man, let alone a man having sex with another man. They said nothing. They said nothing even though some of their former students were out. But they also said nothing about the evils of racism and how negatively women are treated in our communities. There is a prayer that we used to recite at every mass: "Forgive us Lord for what we have done and for what we have failed to do." Repeating that, i always thought that what we did not do could hurt much more than what we did.

When i entered high school, i had mastered how to hide my feelings for men. i knew how to act straight. i knew how to talk about women in derogatory ways that portrayed them as objects instead of people. i knew how to posture and make fun of the boys who didn't fit in. i did this because the last thing i wanted was to be looked at in a different light, which in turn would elicit unwanted questions. It was enough that there were already questions of whether i was Black enough because my parents were white and i didn't look like the typical Black guy. This went on through to grade ten. It even continued into the new school i went to in order to avoid the constant homophobic comments from students and teachers aimed at the students and teachers that were different and didn't fit what was considered normal.

This acting did not end until one day i realized i wasn't being honest with myself to such an extent that i had forgotten who i really was. This scared me. During all these years i had avoided thinking about the feelings i had for men. To do this i hid in the duties and responsibilities of the jobs i worked at. i had worked since i was twelve and worked full time for the last two years of high school.

The day i realized i had forgotten who i was, i went home after classes before i had to go to work, walked into the kitchen and pulled a knife out of the large cedar block on the counter. As i walked down the stairs to my bedroom, the soft scent of the cedar wood reminded me of my grandfather, who had built the block. i laid the knife beside me. i picked up a piece of paper and a pen and thought of all the things i wanted to tell my friends and family. But i simply wrote, "i'm sorry." i lifted the knife to my wrist and as it touched my skin, the phone rang. That was enough to bring me back out of this daze. i told myself that i was allowed one more day to be honest about myself. When i went to work i took my boss aside (she was also the mother of my best friend), and i was honest with her. She said, "That must have been hard to do."

She had no idea.

From that point on, i decided to be honest with my friends and my mother, sister and father. i came out to them in that order. When i began university and learned that my birth mother had been located, it made sense to me that i would be honest with her too. i decided to write her a letter and tell her everything about me even if that meant that i was to never meet her because of it. i sat at my computer and wrote about the work i had done with children, the strength i continued to draw from my parents who were my closest friends, my sister's challenges in life and how that reminded me of the importance of family. i wrote about my plans of a career as a teacher and about my friends.

Telling my birth mother about the people i shared my life with made my hands shake and my heart pound. It was not an easy decision but it was one i needed to make in order to respect myself at that point in my life. One decision along the way. One decision of many....

❖ ❖ ❖

Trials of Education

Jim Lemoire

My art explores the tensions and fluidity of sexual and gender identity formation and expression. Through my work in video and mixed media drawing/photography/painting, I attempt to push the parameters of Canadian queer politics and challenge simplified rhetoric of the mainstream queer liberation movement.

This particular body of work examines the experience of queer youth, who are continually forced to negotiate school life defined by stigma, fear and perhaps anger. I draw on my own personal experiences in the 1980s and early '90s, but also the experiences of the students I teach and those I have met through T.E.A.C.H., both the volunteers and those who attend workshops.

When I began teaching in high schools and sharing stories at T.E.A.C.H., I realized the conversation about equity and the multiple identities of those who identify with the queer community was as much in need as it ever had been! Questions and dialogue drive this work, not answers.

Grade 12 Queer
Video, 2002

This video sarcastically explores the identity and experience of a queer grade twelve student within Canada's educational system. Feelings of exclusion, isolation and nonrepresentation are highlighted through the incongruous relationship between narration and image. The work also raises awareness of the contradictions between the lustful curiosity of sexual identity formation and the internalized homophobia that paradoxically coexists with it.

Scar

Mark Sundal

The letter inviting me, *as a former member of T.E.A.C.H., to write about my experiences as a volunteer now seems much too timely. I was only with the program a short while, although it wasn't because of any problems with the team — they were always supportive and warm. It was short because an awful event convinced me to leave and no longer put myself in the vulnerable, "out there" position of T.E.A.C.H. volunteers confronting homophobia. It was only after a number of years of reflection that I mustered the courage to put into words what had happened, its impact and, most important, what I learned from it. This opportunity to write about why I left T.E.A.C.H. has provided me with the perfect chance to engage in the therapeutic act of writing. So my motivation for writing is to help myself, and perhaps others, through storytelling and sharing. And this is what T.E.A.C.H. is all about: healing ourselves and others through teaching. So here I am, back to tell another T.E.A.C.H. story.*

I have a scar under my right eye, and I still vividly remember the ring that gave it to me. A man spent some time in a bathroom stall describing his ring to me, holding it to my face so that I could clearly see its menacing shape, its sharpness and its golden shimmer in the bleached fluorescence above us. I could feel it break my skin, too, though the adrenaline and crystal meth coursing through me distracted me from any immediate pain I may have felt.

I remember a concrete wall.
I remember the glaze of the porcelain top of the toilet.
I remember my muscles clenching.
I remember that ring so well....

After the cuts had closed and I had finished dousing my mind and body in the drugs I commonly used to quiet my mind and soften my anguish, I was left with a scar. My mark of shame — what felt like a brand saying "homosexual" burned into my face, glaring red for all the world to see. He had marked me "faggot." And rather than wear that mark as a badge of honor, a purple heart for bravery and courage in the face of hate and violence, I wore it as a mark of shame — not for being beaten, and not for refusing to fight back, but for being what he had branded me. The purpose of his action was to coerce me into taking steps backward. And I did.

I should reject the love I felt.
I should reject the desires I wished to fulfill.
I should loathe.
I should hate.
Him. You. Myself.

I had joined T.E.A.C.H. about six months before this. I was very excited about becoming socially active, educating people and the possibility of making life a little easier for young gay people in high school by showing them that there was life after the turmoil of adolescence. I had felt the liberation that came with telling my coming out story to groups of strangers.

But I quit T.E.A.C.H. two weeks after that ring scarred me. I obeyed the fists and took those steps back to a place I did not want to return to, back to a place I did not have to go, though only now do I realize I had a choice then. I was not punched back into the closet. Of course, I was afraid. I know now that most people would have felt that way, but the scar became a constant reminder to me that the right to personal safety and security was not a concern of those who promote hate. When would the next fist full of rings reach from around another corner to coerce me into taking yet more steps backward into fear? All the progress I had made to that point — coming out to my mother, wearing my T-shirt that read, "QUEER AS FUCK," becoming active in the gay community — all those things that made me proud of myself and gave me courage not to be so frightened were erased. I felt vulnerable and paranoid. I became quieter, trying not to give myself away. I stayed home a lot, worrying that certain places I used to frequent might not be safe anymore. Strangers on the street were no longer simply curiosities or part of that sea of interesting people that lived out their interesting and quirky lives in our city. They were watchers. They were sexual police. They were potential assailants, wearing rings. It is only now after a number of years that the exhaustion of this experience has finally brought me out of the shell I'd retreated into.

The few weeks before I decided to submit this story for the T.E.A.C.H. anthology was a period of rapid change for me. I came out to my father, I quit using drugs and I sent an RSVP for my cousin's wedding, confirming my attendance with my *male* date — the typical things that one does when coming out, when finally freeing oneself from the confines of the closet. The strange thing is that I had come out years ago. Well, at least I thought I had. I believed that all the pieces of my story had already been compiled: growing up feeling different, coming out, feeling freedom, pride and love — neat, tidy and now behind me. Good thing, too, because coming out was so uncomfortable, with all the awkward moments, the serious discussions and the vulnerability. I wanted to put it behind me, to get on with living happily and having fun.

But coming out wasn't behind me, and I realize now that it never will be. Stories, by their very nature, are confined by the fact that they must begin and end. Lives can be told as stories but actual lived experiences defy being restricted to such limits. And so today, we continually speak of coming out, telling our coming out story or asking others when they came out, when in fact coming out is not a moment in time at all or even a single story. This story, the catalyst and beginning of my second coming out, is merely one story among a lifetime of stories and, more importantly, a lifetime of coming out. We tend to forget that.

And so, as I tell yet another tale of violence, homophobia, hate, anguish, pain, anger, struggle, healing, growth and hope, we come full circle: coming out, back in, and coming out ... again. I will not pretend that this is a new story. Although I may be accused of being melodramatic, I know that my experience is a variation on a theme. That may be an ordinary theme, but it has yet to become irrelevant. There is something I had not yet learned and so need to reiterate here: Coming out is not a moment in time, not an event, and definitely not a single story, complete with a tidy beginning and end; coming out is a continuing process, a way of life and an ongoing battle. Though I regret losing the years after I left T.E.A.C.H. and hid in my self-constructed prison, I feel that through that loss I have finally learned that this story has to be told. I have a chance to offer something more to T.E.A.C.H. in the shape of this piece of writing and the message it reveals. We are never out. We must always be *coming* out to ensure that we remain strong and defiant against rings that scar and the people who choose to wield them.

◆◆◆

Where Everybody Knows Your Name

Shawn Fowler

I joined T.E.A.C.H. in 1995, had the time of my life, met great people and probably stayed at the party way too long. This was before T.E.A.C.H. became a program of Planned Parenthood of Toronto. On any panel of anti-homophobia educators, I was usually the young one tossed in to liven things up. During T.E.A.C.H. workshops I told two stories that relayed some of the most formative events in my life, one starting early on and the other picking up around high school. People either cracked up at my stories or looked at me in horror and wondered why I was laughing.

When invited to contribute to this anthology, it occurred to me that in all the years I shared this story with countless students and service providers, it had little to do with my dawning sexual awareness, my tearful conversations with family or my first love. It's not my coming out story. It's a story about other people, often strangers, and how they affected my life. It had everything to do with the absolute terror I felt going to school and how it started when I was six and ended when I was fifteen and realized that I was going to leave school dead or alive, and I chose alive. When I joined T.E.A.C.H., the average age of participants was late teens, and I was barely 16. I am amazed that I went into schools then and shared this story, still fresh, with kids who were likely to be engaging in the same activities that made me live in hell.

Lots of T.E.A.C.H. members talk about students or teachers coming out to them in workshops. This never happened to me and I think I know why. I have always been visibly queer. Effeminate, tweezed eyebrows, styled hair, the way I walked, the way I talked: I was a dream of a stereotype. A lot of it was bravado and a shield, but a lot of it I couldn't change, even after countless hours of trying. When people talk about coming out being a choice and an ongoing task, I feel like it's a formality and often something I only do to at least have the dignity of labeling myself. People still feel the need to label me in the same ways they did when I was six, only they usually try to be more polite about it.

I think back to my days in the classroom, and I commiserate with every queenie boy and butch girl. I think it's no wonder that after workshops I would be surrounded by flocks of adolescent girls talking about pop stars or TV shows and not kids coming out, because that would be an act of bravery I cannot conceive. In high school, kids don't skip a beat. Had I, as a workshop participant, gone up to any queer person in any context it would have been an act of confirmation, and I would have been beaten up. Growing up queer in this culture at this time is difficult enough. Being targeted specifically for growing up queer by several hundred people, five days a week for fifteen years is a nightmare. Anyone amazed by statistics of suicide, homelessness and substance abuse among queer youth need only think of it in those terms.

I think I stayed with T.E.A.C.H. for so long, and support the work to this day, because it allowed me the opportunity to heal. When the funny boy came in and bounced around and told his cute story, it was great. But the reality behind the barrettes and one-liners was that I was sixteen, in an alternative school I could never graduate from, already drinking and experimenting with drugs and becoming increasingly isolated from my family. I flirted with homelessness and was lucky enough to have supports to help me through it. T.E.A.C.H. was one of those supports.

I ranted in classrooms just like the ones I ran from as a guest, safe, invited by the school. After a long time, I was able to compress the horrible memories, turning chunks of coal into diamonds of education and experience. My conscious motivation was to help kids in the same shoes I was in, but I think I was really just telling people over and over again that it was okay to be me until I finally believed it myself.

My name is Shawn and this is my story.

I was born and raised in Toronto. Coming out for me wasn't so much about disclosing my sexual orientation. From an early age it was clear to me that others were going to do that for me, probably because they did it so eagerly, so earnestly and so in my face. It also wasn't about packing up my worldly belongings and moving to the big city, because I was already there.

Growing up in the '80s in a working-class neighborhood meant that I spent a lot of time outside. My family lived on a street shared by a lot of other young families, so there were always kids around to play with. I also had an older sister, who was always with me, threatened by my mother, who probably knew that I'd get my ass kicked if I was alone. As a kid I was slight, chatty and daydreamy. I had long hair and spent a lot of time picking flowers and singing the Smurf theme song. It's easy to be cynical and laugh at who I was then, especially looking at pictures — but it's also easy to be ponderous and wonder who I would have become if life had not gotten in the way.

Basically, daydreaming-romantic-oppressed-by-boorish-older-sister boy that I was, I was passionately enamored with Lynda Carter's Wonder Woman. Reruns of her show ran after school and I never missed one. Her outfits, her hair, her crime fighting, her savvy and probably most of all, her spinning transformation from mousy secretary to stunning Amazon with a heart of gold positively mesmerized me. A lot of summer afternoons were spent on Donald Avenue playing out superhero games, and every time it went down the same. My sister and I would get into a knockdown-dragout fight, the kind common among siblings, about who would get to be Wonder Woman. Inevitably, she won with brute strength and I was a sore loser, stuck with being the Hulk or the Green Hornet or something terribly unglam.

So a sweet twist of fate was even sweeter when my mother bought little plastic costume and accessory kits — Wonder Woman and The Hulk — for my sister and me, respectively. The Wonder Woman costume was too small for my sister, and the Hulk's gauntlets were too big for my willowy wrists —the rest is history. For a golden summer, I got to twirl and spin to my heart's content, a happy boy playing in the sunshine.

Around this time, I also noticed that I was becoming a popular target for name-calling. Other kids would call me faggot, gay lord, homo — whatever, and with a six-year-old's insouciance, I brushed it off because, frankly, I had no idea what they were talking about. You can't stay six forever, though, and as the taunts escalated, I eventually clued in to their menacing intent and I changed. I became quiet and shy and spent a lot of time indoors reading and annoying my mom.

It is really hard to be a boy who looks like a girl and who likes to do things other boys don't do, so being a kid was not fun, especially at school. It was like being the only recruit at a boot camp with four hundred loud sergeants. I was miserable. By the time I was eleven I had learned what it meant to live your life one day at a time.

I was streamed into a middle school that organized kids from all over the community into grades seven and eight before sending them to high school. It sounds so melodramatic now, but it was high-stakes drama. The most memorable event was the grade eight locker switch.

Most of my friends were girls, because I felt safe, the oppressed seeking sanctuary or whatever, but it was probably because at that point in my sexual development I still felt boys were gross and was rather indifferent to girls. Or it could have been my unquenchable enthusiasm to discuss New Kids on the Block, the original boy band. Anyway, school administration had assigned lockers along a really long hallway. That boys were on one side, girls on the other did not become apparent to me until one day at lunch. The principal walked down to the hallway teeming with preteens and came up to me. He calmly explained that I had mistakenly assumed ownership of the wrong locker, something I should have noticed since I was the only boy on the girl's side. As a result, I had to pack up all of my stuff, including a locker mirror and New Kids posters, march it across the hall and take a new locker, surrounded by boys who thought it was hilarious that the fag thought he was a girl and was getting his comeuppance. Meanwhile, I was also the only boy who had elected to stay in family studies in grade eight and I had to carry my half-sewn stuffed animal project too. I remember walking from the lockers into the washroom (I made sure it was the boys') and crying in a stall, tears flowing because every day, everything was so damned hard. I also harbored secret hopes that Danny Wood would sweep me off my feet to his palatial Boston home to the insane jealousy of all my classmates; this just demonstrates to me that I never lost perspective. This retelling of the events is pure Judy Blume angst, but when they happened I wanted to die. I didn't care if my bladder emptied onto the floor or what outfit I was to be buried in, I wanted to be dead.

By the time I entered high school, I thought I had seen it and heard it all. I was wrong.

I went to a mainstream high school for three years. I was a classic disassociated student. I skipped classes, was sullen, walked close to walls with my head hung low — basically I was Ally Sheedy in *The Breakfast Club*. I tried to make myself inconspicuous, so I dyed my hair black and pledged my allegiance to pagan gods and '60s rock. Somehow this made sense back then.

Daily abuse built up in the hallways, classrooms, the caf, and at one point I felt like even the curriculum was a set-up: The same teacher who tolerated students shouting names at me in her classroom actually assigned me to a media arts project on AIDS in America. Why not just set me on fire in the courtyard?

I was slugging blindly through, having come out to my family in a bizarre twist of events that involved my snooping mother, my deaf grandmother, a Marilyn Monroe wig and Pauly Shore. I was fourteen and working at a summer camp. One Friday afternoon, my mother, concerned that I was so withdrawn and quiet, went through my bedroom looking for crack pipes or something. She discovered a rollerblade box in my closet. She opened the box and discovered the implements for my grand plan to bust into gay Toronto.

I was spending a lot of time with my friend Tammy that summer. She was older, she had a boyfriend with a car and she smoked. How could I not love her? The boyfriend was another story. (Driven to desperation because Tammy and I endlessly mugged to RuPaul's "Supermodel" in his back seat, he ran over my cassette and restricted his car playlist to Depeche Mode. Ew.)

Tammy also had a friend, Shon, who was gay and had a life. She partied with him at gay bars like Boots and Colby's, and I listened in awe and amazement to her stories of line dancing to the Pet Shop Boys. Faster than you can say, "Go Wessssssssssssst," that awe turned into envy and desperation. I finally disclosed my sexual orientation to her in the back of her boyfriend's car, and the plotting began. We had no idea that there was an actual queer community at this point, so we thought my "in" would be a bar. But I was so young. Hmm. We spent endless hours poring over *People* and *Tiger Beat* until finally, revelation was upon us: I would go in drag. Drag queens were timeless, elegant, mysterious and very cosmopolitan creatures in the early '90s and I was going to be one.

We set about assembling my outfit. Makeup came from my mother's Mary Kay samples, shoes from some skeezy store on Yonge Street, panty hose disappeared from the washing machine and we got a Marilyn Monroe wig from Shoppers Drug Mart. The pièce de resistance was a black stretch velvet dress I "sent for dry cleaning" for my sister.

My mother, thinking I was using drugs, opened the rollerblade box, and instead of finding needles and spoons, she found heels and hair. Uh-oh.

She immediately called my grandmother and told her that she had discovered that I wanted a sex change. My grandmother blabbed to my entire family that I was becoming a woman, and my sister took off to reclaim her dress. Meanwhile, I was playing double Dutch at work, and had no idea what was going on.

After work, when I arrived at my grandmother's for dinner, it immediately registered that my brothers and father were looking at me strangely. I thought, "Okay — I must have left some face paint on or something," so I went to the bathroom to check. Precisely then, my sister, the queen of tact, walked upstairs in her dress and heels. *Eeek!* I rushed to the phone and made plans with the first person I could get in touch with, my friend Jeannine, and I ran out of the house to go see *In The Army Now*, starring Pauly Shore.

My father insisted on driving me. He gave me a speech on the way to the subway, saying that he loved me and accepted me, warning me that my mother thought I was a transsexual and encouraging me to be strong, as I was to face a difficult life of people judging me. What?? I would have participated in this conversation and pointed out that a difficult life of judgment was nothing new, but I was trying to throw myself out the window. A conversation with my father at that point in my life was hard enough, but one about my sexual orientation? Total disaster!

I went to the movies and stayed out as late as possible, but eventually headed home. I felt like Frodo — each challenge was more difficult than the last, but my journey was my fate. Is it vain to think you're the chosen one? I walked up to my house, thanked God that all of the lights were out and my family appeared to be sleeping, and crept to my room. I was almost at my door when a sliver of light appeared. My drama queen mother appeared backlit in her bedroom doorway and asked me to come and sit with her.

I was quaking. My mother was a force to be reckoned with, and I was a mama's boy through and through. She sat on her bed and beckoned me to sit. Her duvet was scattered with tissues, crumpled with a thousand disappointments and mascara. She looked at me with heartbreaking earnestness, and told me that if I ever needed panty hose or lingerie, she would take me shopping.

What?!?

Scanning over the last few hours, I put two and two together and realized my mother thought my stash of drag stuff meant I was a budding transsexual, not a resourceful and cunning young gay man trying to bust onto the scene. I quickly clarified the situation for her, and I think she was a bit disappointed that we would not be going onto *Maury Povich* (gay teens were done, transsexuals were the rage on the talk show circuit). Things with Mom were a bit tense after that, but fine.

My mother vetoed the bar plan. A year later, after numerous failed attempts to find Church Street downtown that ended up with me lost at Queen's Park, I discovered supports through Toronto's queer community. So while my soul was being crushed in school five days a week, I was out every night stretching my wings and dancing, talking and living a life with friends I didn't have to castrate myself for and who liked me for exactly the same thing I was being punished for: my queerness. I was funny, fun and for the first time in a long time, I liked myself. Actually, I still hated myself but was too busy having fun to remember. So against all likelihood, I had gone out and gotten myself some self-esteem, which proved a dangerous and unlikely mix with York Memorial Collegiate Institute. In grade eleven, what proved to be my last year in a mainstream high school, I arrived at school one morning and walked to my locker. The aisle in which my locker was situated had been vandalized. In thick black marker, someone had written numbers, the usual high school "I ♥ Satan" stuff, and on my locker, "fag," "faggot," "die," "go home" and other charming niceties. I stood in front of my locker, shaking. I had a physical reaction to such a tangible and vivid expression of hate that was aimed at me and condoned by the institution where I was supposed to be nurtured and educated. The worst part of the experience was seeing this for the first time and being surrounded by classmates, "friends," who laughed and carried on their lives as usual, ignorant of the fact that my life had been changed forever. I will never forget them talking about Donna getting drunk at prom on *90210* while my head spun. Burning with shame, I left the school and headed home, vowing never to return.

My mother immediately sent me back with no excuse note, so I called my older sister, now living with my grandmother because she was wild and uncontrollable, and asked her to come with me. So, armed with a posse of rocker chicks with cigarettes in their cleavage and Guns N' Roses T-shirts, I went into my vice principal's office and explained to her why I had left and asked her what she was going to do to help me. She gave me a new locker, told me there was no policy to deal with something of this nature and shuffled me off, asking my hardass chick posse to evacuate the premises ASAP. In retrospect, with the administration so clearly out of touch with the needs of the student body, it is no surprise to me that the school was plagued by weird acts of resistance, like someone ditching random animal parts in the library that were discovered when they started to stink.

Keenly aware that I was alone and no one was going to help me, I left York Memorial at the end of that year with my yearbook under my arm. I was such a mess from my experience at York Memo, I cried when I told the same "friends" who ignored me that morning at my locker that I wasn't returning in September. No one followed my wistful yearbook directions to call me over the summer, written in a faggy, loopy cursive.

During the course of the year, I had discovered a support group for students in the Toronto School Board who were queer. I started going to meetings and heard about a new school program that was going to open the following school year, a classroom designed to be a safe space for queer kids who were victimized in mainstream schools. Blindly ignoring the flashing red lights in my head, I enrolled, and in one fell swoop went against sixteen years of intense conditioning and made a decision without maternal input. I spent the entire summer dodging questions about what classes I had selected for the upcoming year, but my mother intercepted the information package mailed to me from the Triangle Program. Calling her reaction dramatic would be a massive understatement. She screamed, she yelled, she threatened to call Social Services and have me committed, but I stood firm. I was not going to any school other than Triangle. Eventually a compromise was reached: basically I signed away all my leisure time and babysat my brothers in return for bus fare.

I started at Triangle and joined T.E.A.C.H. the following fall.

"Queer a Space ...Woman of Color Coming Through!"

Elysha Mawji

I initially joined T.E.A.C.H. so that I could tell my story in the hopes of making a silent connection with someone struggling through the loneliness that I had long felt. I've finally reached a point in my life where I feel comfortable living in my body as a queer woman of color and am now itching to engage in dialogue about the issues surrounding queer youth like myself. It's vitally important to me to let others know that queer people of color do exist in the community. In this manner, I feel like I'm giving voice and presence to an often invisible group. Since joining T.E.A.C.H. this fall, I have learned and unlearned a tremendous amount from both co-facilitators and workshop participants about the ways in which we can dismantle homophobic and heterosexist views. I find that I am continuously being challenged by difficult questions and comments in the workshops. These challenges then force me to think more critically and allow me to see the material being discussed from different vantage points. To me the most

exhilarating part of facilitating T.E.A.C.H. workshops has been
learning alongside co-facilitators and participants how to think and act
more creatively when challenging myopic views around gender and
sexual diversity.

Ever since I can remember, I've always been sexually and emotionally attracted to women and not men. All through primary school and ever since, I've known this about myself. When I was very young I knew that this was natural and right, but as I went through primary school and into high school, I thought there was something wrong with me. Everyone around me seemed to be romantically inclined toward members of the opposite sex only. To this end, I kept my feelings locked up inside throughout high school.

In grade nine, I was in a sex education class where the topic was homosexuality. At one point during the class, the teacher started to read out statistics and said that 10 percent of our population is gay and lesbian. I quickly scanned the room. There were about thirty of us there that day. I remember thinking: Did that mean that two other people there were either gay or lesbian? And then I realized that maybe others were looking around and thinking the same thing. This frightened me, so I looked down at my desk and hoped that no one suspected me.

From that moment on, I decided to hide my feelings and true self for good. I hoped that I'd blend in as a straight person and that no one would ever suspect me. No one did. I managed to suppress my natural romantic desires and needs all through high school, distracting myself with sports, clubs and academics. The fact that

I really loved school helped me in this endeavor. No one at my high school was openly gay or lesbian or bisexual, so it just became a non-issue.

When I went on to university, I was exposed to a much larger community that wasn't at all homogeneous like my high school. People seemed to stand out more as separate and distinct entities. For the first time, I saw visible signs acknowledging the existence of queer people. I saw rainbow stickers on people's office doors and residence rooms with the words lesbian, gay, bisexual, transsexual and queer on them. And I noticed that these people posted their stickers and signs with positive attitudes.

This frightened me at first because these signs and people started to reawaken my true feelings and thoughts about myself. I began to meet people who were openly gay or lesbian or queer and seemed to be fine with it. Still, I thought how daunting it would be to have to face all my friends and family who had known me for so long and explain to them something new about myself. It frightened me and made me tired just thinking about it.

But I was thinking about it. In fact, the more I became exposed to queer people and issues and stickers, the more I thought about it. And soon I was feeling very trapped and uneasy again. I felt that there was a part of me that was tied up inside me and wanted to be let out. I felt something beating against my insides and pleading with me to be let free. I wanted to be free to talk about my feelings and thoughts. I wanted my friends and family and people around me to know me for me, and most important I wanted to meet a girl like me and kiss her and hold her hand.

By the end of my first year, I decided to tell my best friend that

I was gay. And that's exactly what I told her. We were outside the Royal Ontario Museum and I was demolishing a bush next to our bench by pulling off the little needles one by one and breaking them into smaller bits. This was all I could do to keep myself from shaking. My eyes were watery, and I had a hard time looking her in the eye while I told her. Once I did, I felt a mixture of nausea and relief. She looked right at me without flinching and told me that she loved me and that I was one of the coolest people she knew. She hugged me and assured me that she didn't think of me any differently, so this experience ignited a confidence in me that enabled me to tell other friends that I was queer.

Over the next year, I came out to most of my friends and even to my parents and sister. With each person that I told, a new wave of relief would come over me. I cried a lot during this time out of fear and happiness and confusion. For me, telling the people I loved that I was gay or lesbian or queer was a very cathartic process. The type of cry I often had wasn't a quiet shedding of tears but rather a loud and messy, physically tiring spewing out of emotions that had been kept inside me for far too long. As I went through this process, little by little my sick and ill feelings dissipated and were replaced by feelings of relief and contentment. I began to feel comfortable with my thoughts and feelings and felt happy to be in my body.

During my second and third years of university, I started to seek out people who were like me and found support and friends within the queer community. I also began avidly reading about queer issues. While all this was going on in my life, I was also heavily involved in my university community. I was elected to the student council and participated in various school and community events. In my fourth year I became a don/residence assistant and continued on my student council. I was thoroughly enjoying my university experience as an out, brown, queer woman.

Then one day early on in my fourth year, I came across a flyer for a queers-of-color group on campus. I was very excited and wanted to go and find out what the group was all about. "I'm brown/South Asian and queer," I thought to myself, "I wonder if there are other queer South Asians out there too?" As I jotted the date of the meeting in my calendar, I started thinking about who I would rope in to attend this event with me. I began to make a mental list of all my queer-identified friends and my friend Justin was the first person to pop into my head. Without giving it a second thought, I called him up and invited him to come along. Justin laughed and said that he'd love to come except for the fact that he was white and that it was a queers-of-color group. He was right. I couldn't believe that I hadn't realized that. I knew he was queer, but he certainly was white and not a person of color. This really gave me a shock and made me stop and think. I went back to my mental list of queer friends and realized that not one of them was a person of color. This thought both confused and frightened me.

A couple of weeks later, with all these perplexing thoughts in my head, I attended a conference hosted by Ryerson University, York University and the University of Toronto called Bent on Change. The theme of the conference was "Beyond Tolerance: Rethinking Queer Issues on Campus and in Communities." It was an excellent conference and I took away many things. The most important thing I learned was that within the queer community there are many other communities that are even more isolated, estranged and invisible, "minorities within minorities." One of these communities is queer people of color. I learned that, yes, queer people of color do exist! And I learned that many people often think to themselves that people of color couldn't possibly have diverse sexual orientations because they're already Black or South Asian or East Asian. I learned that people who identify as queer people of color are really an invisible group in our community at large.

And then I learned that one of the ways to make this community more visible and less estranged and to erase people's misconceptions and allow them to unlearn them, would be for people who identify as queers of color to take up space. By this I mean that queer people of color like myself could choose to be recognized as queer people of color doing just what they do in their everyday lives and positions. I heard many queer people of color at the conference say things like, "Yeah, we need to become visible and take up space," or, "We need to start taking up prominent positions or positions of power in society and show ourselves so that people can see that we exist and that we are just like everyone else," or, "We need to be seen so that we can act as role models for other queers of color so that they also know that we exist." And so after the conference I went home and thought about it. And I thought, "we," as queer people of color, do take up space, and we do act as role models.

Then it really struck me: I didn't know one single queer person of color up until a couple of weeks ago. Although I knew many people who identified as queer, not one was a person of color. And then I thought, wait a minute, we are here, but we *are* invisible. The invisibility concern was in fact warranted. I decided that I wanted to do something about this and be a part of the change that I want and need to see, so I decided to make a motion at a University College student council meeting to begin the process of change.

This moment in my life was both exciting and scary because of its significance as a formal commitment on my part to perform change. The student council to which I proposed this formal motion is the oldest university student government in Canada and so this was a big deal to me. I was petrified, but when it came to my turn to give my formal report for the month, I addressed the Speaker and asked if I could make a motion. He agreed, and with a trembling voice I read my motion to the council of over 30 members: "Be it resolved that this year's 2002–03 Lit Outreach Commissioner, Elysha Mawji, be formally recognized as a queer person of color who is taking up space on her university campus."

After making my motion I waited in silence for what seemed like an eternity. All background noise seemed to fade away and all I heard was silence. I then saw the speaker mouthing a question, asking for a seconder to my motion, and out of the corner of my eye I saw my friend Jessie's hand shoot up into the air. Then, "All those in favor of the motion?... All those opposed?... All those abstaining?" Still, I couldn't hear a thing. Silence. By this time I was looking down at the table. Then all of a sudden thirty to forty hands were banging on the Croft Chapter House table in approval of the motion. The motion passed unanimously and again I felt a wave of relief come over me, but this time it was accompanied by a feeling of pride.

Since that time I have tried to be an activist in my community by taking up space as a queer woman of color. To me, taking up space simply means being out as the queer woman of color that I am in the spaces in which I live, work and play. In so doing, I continue to be engaged in the process of learning and unlearning that relates to queer issues.

Whole

Stephen Wei

I've told this story *many times in numerous formats, editing out pieces here and pieces there. When I tell my story to a straight audience, either to friends or at T.E.A.C.H. workshops, it is purely a coming out story, and the issue of race doesn't figure very prominently. When I tell it to gay white men, race is at the forefront, and it surprises and educates many of them to issues they have been blind to. When I share it with gays of color, there are usually two reactions: the first is a sense of solidarity in the double oppression we face; the second is one of denial that the issue of racism within the gay community even exists.*

I always knew I was different.

I mean, my hair was jet black, my eyes were different, and my parents spoke a different language than everybody else. How much different than all the white kids could you get?

In grade three, four boys backed me into a corner of the school during recess, then told me, "Go back to where you came from," called me a "chink" and bullied me for most of that year. In grade four, I was chased home from school by a group of boys who yelled their imitation of Chinese words at my Asian friends and me.

I was an outsider. I hated being Chinese. I hated my squat, ugly nose, my thin, single-lidded eyes, and my parents' inability to speak English. I refused to learn Chinese. I told my mother to make "real" food instead of Chinese food all the time. I distanced myself from all the Chinese kids who had newly immigrated; I called them FOBs (Fresh off the Boats) just like everybody else did. I ran from racist persecution by making these kids targets of my own, by ostracizing them and insisting that they were the ones who were different, not me, because they were still Chinese and I was not.

After a while the racism I faced died away. I was just another kid until I went to junior high school in grade seven. Then I wasn't persecuted for being Chinese. Instead, it was because I was the scrawny loser who hadn't hit puberty. I hit the beginning of an arduous seven-year awkward phase. It's the same old story: I was the last to be picked for teams, I got beaned in the head with every conceivable type of ball and stick and the only kids who would tolerate me were the girls.

I actually wore the role of a pre-puberty boy with pride, initially. It was a huge joke that I hadn't hit puberty yet and that's why I didn't like girls. I kept wondering when I'd eventually like them. I asked everybody I knew, "How will I know when I like a girl that way?" Everybody's answer was, "Oh, you'll know."

Of course, I never did.

In high school, I started to truly rebel against the aspects of my identity I so despised. My awkwardness and my lack of machismo branded me an outsider from the realm of boys. I fled to the safety of the drama club. In running to this safe place and away from the teenaged testosterone of phys ed, I was also running away from what I saw as Chinese stereotypes. I reviled math and revelled in the arts.

I was embraced by this incredibly liberal fold. Despite this aura of acceptance, I began doing my best to pretend I liked girls, often even convincing myself as well. Within the protective halo that my drama friends offered, I eventually stopped having to pretend. I stopped feeling the need to convince myself I liked girls. In time, I came to the revelation that there was yet another layer of difference in me. I didn't like girls — I loved men. While the usual angst over this issue ensued, it wasn't nearly as crippling as my friends' own angst over their breakups, teenage political dramas and acne breakouts. I was centered. I realized who I was, and I was happy.

I was happy except with the person I saw in the mirror. When I looked in the mirror I saw something ugly, because I still didn't like who I was. I felt I needed a masculine, white man to make me feel beautiful. I met my first boyfriend in my last year of high school. He was seven years older than I was and in university. He was white; actually he was Jewish, but in my eyes, just another Caucasian guy. Everything about us created a power difference between the two of us. He was in university, I was in high school, so I often deferred to his interpretation of things. He was white, I was Asian, so I often felt that he was the more valuable partner in the relationship. On at least one occasion I referred to him as the "man" in the relationship. This is probably why he wasn't the best person for me.

In time, I learned of the stereotypes of gay Asian men. I learned that we were all labeled as effeminate bottoms. Asian men who were attracted to other Asian men were often called lesbians by their own community. I immediately rejected this idea. I didn't want anybody to think that I was a girly-boy anymore. I had had enough of all that in junior high, so I started to take kung fu.

And it was this choice that made me realize how insane my life was. I was fleeing the stereotype of the gay Asian girly-boy by taking kung fu. I can't think of anything more ass-backward. I became a drama fag when I escaped my Chinese stereotypes. I had made fun of the FOBs to avoid the racism directed at me for being Chinese. Despite this pattern, I accepted being gay, but I still couldn't deal with what people saw when they saw the color of my skin.

Coming out for me wasn't really hard. There were moments of self-doubt and initially I wanted to be straight so badly that I would lie in bed praying to a God I really didn't believe in to strip me of all that made me gay. It was having supportive friends around me who loved me for who I was that made it easy to accept myself. Coming out to my family held its own drama, which played out positively. When my mother found out, she cried for a week. She got over it, and to this day she still supports me. When I told my father, he told me to just "stop doing it." When I told him it wasn't as simple as that, he replied with an affirmation of love and practicality: "Oh, fine. Well, you're my son and I love you. Don't worry about it."

What was harder for me was dealing with being Chinese. It wasn't until I started working with the queer organization at York University when I was a student there that I started to realize that all the internalized homophobia that others suffer was the same as the internalized racism I faced. The more I came to understand why I should be proud to be gay, the more I realized that I should be proud to be Asian too.

I joined T.E.A.C.H. near the end of my university career, and it was the work of teaching against homophobia that led me to realize that I still needed to do so much to teach against racism too. It was at T.E.A.C.H. that I learned to make these connections. I don't believe that the teaching of anti-homophobia can be separated from the teaching of anti-racism, anymore than it can be separate from sexism, transphobia, classism or any of the other hundreds of ways that we as the human race seek to divide ourselves and oppress anyone who is "different."

I used to wonder whether I would have been as aware of racism if I hadn't dealt with homophobia and as ready to fight homophobia if I hadn't faced racism. In the end, I suppose the question is irrelevant because I cannot compartmentalize myself so easily. I am a Chinese, gay, middle-class man with all my oppressions and privileges rolled together. They are all facets of who I am; together they make me whole.

✦✦✦

I used to be a ghost ...

Jenn F.

At T.E.A.C.H., *we have two kinds of volunteers: peer facilitators and support volunteers. Facilitators have the incredibly hard job of standing up in front of groups of their peers and throwing themselves open emotionally so that they can try to break down people's hatred, misperceptions and misinformation. As a support volunteer, I'm there to help them do whatever they need to do. Sometimes I talk to classes, other times I'm just a friend/den mother who helps make things happen. We laugh together. We cry together. And we love our work. Unfortunately, I don't get to tell my story as often as I'd like but having heard other people's, I know that stories can be powerful things. Things that change your view of the world. This is mine....*

When you were little, what did you dream of being when you grew up? a doctor who saved people's lives? an astronaut who explored far out into space? or maybe a famous singer who sang the kinds of songs that made people laugh or weep? I didn't want to be any of those things. I just wanted to be a normal little girl and maybe a mommy some day. That shouldn't be too big a dream, should it?

It was turning into a really good summer ... I wasn't in school yet, so the days had that wonderful way of running together the way they do when you're young and don't know about the world "out there."

Her name was June and she was my very, very bestest friend ever. We would have tea parties, play hide-and-go-seek and hold bake sales with stuff we'd make in her Easy-Bake oven. That year we played a game that what was all the rage with the girls on the block: We did tricks with buttercups to test and see if we were *really in love* with so-and-so from around the corner (smile). You could lie but the buttercup *always* told the truth! We were so close that it went without saying that when she told me she was having another sleepover, this time with her friends from Brownies, I was included. I mean ... how could I not? We'd never missed each other's sleepovers our entire lives!

That's when I found out that I was different.

It seemed that I wasn't allowed to join in because I wasn't a girl like all the rest of them. "Of course I am!" I protested loudly when Mom and Dad tried to explain it to me. Parents could be so silly sometimes. Truth be known, June and I had already discussed our differences in anatomy but we'd dismissed it as just "one of those things." Her belly button was an "outie" and mine was an "innie." Her crotch had an "innie" and I had an "outie." It just made sense that both our respective "outies" would just drop off at some point and then everything would be okay. But things weren't going to be okay. Not then ... and not for a very, very long time.

A couple of months later when we started school, June began to treat me differently. At school it was "us" and "them" and apparently I was suddenly a "them," much to my dismay and protests. I was told that I was no longer in "the club" and that I didn't belong. I knew they were wrong but that isn't much consolation when you're five years old. Later, I told my parents that I wanted to join Brownies. Instead, they sent me to Boy Scouts. "Be good for him to socialize with other boys," they said. "Toughen him up." I went once and was so terrified that I cowered in the corner for most of the evening. I knew that I didn't fit in, and worse, the others knew too.

That's when I learned to start hiding.

We moved away a year later and I lost touch with June, but I never forgot how much fun we used to have together until I became a "them" ... a boy in her and the rest of society's eyes. I remember crying a lot. Crying and hiding....

Then, when I was eight years old, I cut my hip on a rusty old fence and got a very nasty infection. I didn't want to be a bother or complain. Boys didn't do that. They just toughed it out. So that's what I did ... for almost three weeks before the infection got so bad that I lost the use of my right leg entirely. Then I couldn't hide it anymore. "Umm ... I can't come downstairs for dinner Mom. I ... umm ... can't walk.... No, no, no ... just ignore me. I'm fine. Really!"

North York General Hospital. Room 412. I was in traction there for almost three weeks and managed to make lots of friends with the nurses and staff. Sure, I missed Halloween but to cheer me up, a volunteer gave me a little blue bunny rabbit to mark the occasion. My roommate got a cowboy. God understood even if no one else did. He hadn't made my "outie" drop off so that I'd be like the other girls but he had made sure that I got the cute bunny and not some rotten cowboy. I took some small measure of consolation from that. This was a small affirmation in an otherwise dismal existence.

It was a Sunday afternoon in mid-November when he came in. I don't recall his name but I'll never forget his face. He was a youth volunteer who came around once in a while to visit patients and try to cheer them up. We'd sort of become friends, so he was excited that I was finally out of traction, although still confined to bed for a few more days. We talked about this and that, and then he got onto the topic of wishes.

Sixteen-year-old boy: So, if you could wish for anything, what would it be?

Eight-year-old Jenn: Umm ... chocolate ice cream?

Sixteen-year-old boy: Oh come on. Think bigger! You're a boy. How about a sexy girl friend? Or a really hot car to cruise around in and pick up chicks?

Eight-year-old Jenn: Umm ... no ... I don't think so. I'm okay with ice cream.

Sixteen-year-old boy: Oh come on ... there must be something that you really, really want more than anything else in the whole world?

This went on for a few minutes, back and forth. He'd push. I'd demurely decline to state my wish. He'd push. Finally I said it.

And my world changed forever. I started pleadingly. By the end I was screaming and I kept screaming for a long time after that.

Eight-year-old Jenn: (sullen) You can't give me what I want.

Sixteen-year-old boy: Oh, come on. What do you want more than anything else?

Eight-year-old Jenn: I need someone to fix me. To make me a girl like I should have been.

Sixteen-year-old boy: WHAT DID YOU JUST SAY?!?

Eight-year-old Jenn: I'm wrong. I need someone to fix me.

Sixteen-year-old boy: YOU FREAK! F***ING PERVERT! YOU SICK LITTLE...!!!

Eight-year-old Jenn: I KNOW they can fix me! I KNOW!! I KNOW!!

Sixteen-year-old boy: YOU PERVERTED LITTLE SACK OF SH*T!! I OUGHTA BEAT THE LIVING **** OUT OF YOU, YOU PERVERT!!

Eight-year-old Jenn: I NEED THEM TO FIX ME!! I KNOW THEY CAN FIX ME!! PLEASE TALK TO THEM FOR ME?!?

Sixteen-year-old boy: You better just stop that kinda talk right now, you perverted little homo! Do you KNOW what they do to people like you, you f***ing pervert? Keep that kinda talk up and they'll come and take you away and you'll never see any of your friends or family ever again! They'll lock you up in a little padded room and give you needles and pills and electric shocks and, darn it, they'll make a boy out of you or kill you trying! How would you like that, huh?... HUH?!?

Eight-year-old Jenn: Why won't you fix me? I KNOW YOU CAN!! PLEASE!! PLEASE!! I NEED YOU TO FIX ME!!!

This went on for what seemed like forever until the nurses came and dragged him out of the room. With my tormentor gone, I threw myself face down under my pillows, bawled my eyes out and prayed to God in my most sincere eight-year-old voice to "Please, please, take me to be with the angels." I didn't know what the word "suicide" meant but I knew that I wanted to die right there and then because I couldn't take it anymore. Not one day more.

The nurses stopped talking to me after that.

Two days later I learned what true terror was. I was sent to see a woman in a white coat who wanted to ask me some things. She seemed very nice but I worried that if I answered any of her questions the wrong way that they'd take me away and do horrible things to me. So I stared at the floor and kept repeating the same words over and over again.

"My name is Michael and I promise to be a good boy."

She asked some more questions and I continued to stare at the floor.

"My name is Michael and I promise to be a good boy."

After what seemed like an eternity, she let me go back to my room and I hid under the covers, crying, waiting for them to take me away. I prayed again for the angels to save me before the bad people came and made me a boy. But the angels never came and I was discharged a couple of days later. The hospital staff told my parents nothing and I certainly wasn't talking.

Years passed and I worked very, very hard at being that good little boy. I went to a prestigious all-boys school, mostly for the education, but also because my parents felt that I needed more male influence in my life.

I continued to hide.

I knew I didn't fit in and if I ever forgot that painful fact, there were twelve hundred guys around, most of whom were more than willing to "educate" me. The taunts, the jeers, the ostracism, the sexual victimization.... I got out of school and went on to complete a university degree and get a good job.

I was still hiding.

People didn't see me. I was now a ghost who came to work, said little and never let anyone get close, because if they did ... I might let something slip, and as I'd been taught too many times in the past, *that* was dangerous.

Eventually I started to tell girlfriends about myself ... about Jenn. It usually went surprisingly well ... all things considered.

Jenn: Umm ... Tish? *(biting upper lip)* I umm ... I want to be your girlfriend.

Tish: But you're a guy ... and you're my boyfriend.

Jenn: Don't let looks deceive you, hon.

Tish: What exactly are you talking about?

Jenn: I'm umm ... I'm really a girl inside.

Tish: Yeah ... right! *(laughs and giggles)* You are so crazy!

Jenn: No ... really! You just can't make this kind of stuff up! *(sweet innocent smile)*

Tish: Hmm ... well ... I do love the different dynamic that we have in our relationship. And you sure aren't like any of the other guys that I've ever dated. *(thoughtful look)* OK, but does that mean that I get to be the boy in the relationship, if I want to?

Jenn: Sure, we can do that or what about if we tried swapping around roles?

Tish: Sure. That sounds kewl. Come here. *(sly smile)*

I tried really hard to make that work ... and it did for a long time. But eventually it just wasn't enough. I hated the body I saw in the mirror. It wasn't me!! Maybe I hadn't always had a name for what I was feeling/going through, but that hadn't made the pain of gender dysphoria any easier to handle. I also hated the way I'd found to deal with it ... by trying my absolute hardest to make everybody else happy at my own expense. I couldn't handle it any more. Not by a long shot.

So I got on the Internet and started searching. I read personal pages, found online resources and chat rooms, and I realized that I was not alone. I started to go out and socialize. I found community. I found pride. And in all of this I was learning what it was to just be me, the person I'd hidden away from so many people for so long, and surprisingly enough, people honestly seemed to like me and wanted to spend time with me.

And then I transitioned and life got even better.

I used to be a ghost, you see, but now I've joined those who help light the candle and dispel the darkness.

My name is Jenn and I'm a woman who enjoys the love of some very special friends and who tries to give back to those who are coming behind me by volunteering for T.E.A.C.H. I want to put a human face on the word "transsexual" ... to challenge the perceptions of those who think it's a dirty word and to be a role model for those who question whether they might be one as well.

I've finally had my dream granted. What about yours?

◆◆◆

What's your birthname?

M. Francino

This is not *the story I tell at T.E.A.C.H. workshops. I'm telling this
story instead for three reasons. First, "What's your birthname?" is the
question I am asked the most during the question period. The audience
always seems more interested in how one physically transitions and
what name my birthparents bestowed upon me. Most of my co-
facilitators get inquiries that pertain specifically to their stories, such as
"How have your parents dealt with your coming out since?" or "So at
what age exactly did you know?" I used to not discuss my name in my
T.E.A.C.H. story. It was never a key element in my complicated identity
struggle. My chosen name really found me quite easily and I remember
the ease with which I switched names. Yet, workshop after workshop,
the questions kept dealing with this mysterious unmentioned birthname
that everyone just had to find out about. Second, I am currently in the
process of rewriting my story for the nth time. The first story I wrote for
this anthology dealt with my coming out as a dyke, because at the time
that was all I was comfortable doing. Then I just couldn't help but tag*

on the continuation of my story when I came back out to both my friends and myself as a tranny boi. This was unsatisfactory, however, for many reasons. My original story dealt with how I came to understand and accept my loving people of the same birthsex, not how I came to accept my true gender identity. Third, because I am by no means the only tranny who has a mixed relationship with their name. Telling people has backfired all too often and has led to more hardship than was conceivable beforehand. So I want to deal with this, and I feel this anthology is a good place to begin. The piece is for all those who ask to know my birthname and probably don't realize what it says about them. It's for all those who more than likely don't understand what it is that they wind up really asking me, because that question is never a simple one for this tranny. This piece is about everything that is never directly said in the workshop by the audience and all the replies I will never have the courage or opportunity to put forth.

What's your birthname?

Translation number 1:

I'm trying to picture your original self; I need to in order to be able to judge how well you are doing according to my personal requirements for passing.

What's your birthname?

Translation number 2:

If I can't picture the real you, I will be distressed. I mean you were born as a girl and I must see you that way.

What's your birthname?

Translation number 3:

Honest curiosity at first, with no ill intent; just, what killed the cat?

(Once you're told, that may change. You may find yourself picturing the birthme or trying to analyze my choice of name. Or telling you my birthname may lead to further questions that will have these effects.)

What's your birthname?

Translation number 4:

I need you to tell me to prove to me that you believe me when I say I respect you. I mean, you should be able to confide in me this piece of information, which I keep telling you is so benign, though don't point out to me that it obviously is of outmost importance to me. That might just make me think about my own insecurities around similar issues.

What's your birthname?

Answer you will never hear:

You don't know what you are asking of me. It isn't that simple a question. But if I don't answer it, you will decide I'm a jerk. If I do answer, you will either begin to slips and call me by a name that was mine but was never me or you will just outright bash me.

What's your birthname?

Answer you will never hear:

I have to wonder where your question is coming from. Why do you care? Why do you need so much to see the original me? I'm doing my best to pass; it may or may not be succeeding, but that's the best I can do. You can never fully comprehend what's at stake for me, nor should you need to.

What's your birthname?

Answer you will never hear:

I don't care why you're asking. Here's what you don't know and I'm not allowed to say for countless reasons you would never believe anyway. It doesn't matter what it was. It died a brutal and painful death. I *hate* my birthname. There is so much pain and hatred attached to it, you wouldn't believe. If I choose to say it, in specific contexts, it's totally fine. But my name is what betrayed me as a baby, it's what made people look at me twice throughout childhood, and it's what gives me away now more often than anything else. It's this curse that follows me around despite my best intentions. Every time it was muttered in the past, negative things ensued. I was outed, I stopped passing, name it. At home, in privacy, my parents only called me that when I screwed up. It was my daily/hourly reminder of the limitations to both my sex and self when uttered by profs, peers, you name it. It was this horrid thing slapped on to me. It caused my mother so much grief because of the way it was always mispronounced by anglophones, and all the bullshit around that aspect of it is completely unrelated to transsexuality.

What's your birthname?

Answer you will never hear:

It is an easy way to deflect topics that are harder for you to face, such as whether any or all of this applies to you. But let's focus on me? That way my name, my gender, is clearly a personal condition that pertains only to me. Your gender is not in question, surely. My name does not require a doctor or grasping of concepts beyond those you already had before I spoke to you today. It's a safe topic to approach that has surely never been considered by others for the sole purpose of seeming trans-friendly while not resorting to outright avoidance of the topic.

What's your birthname?

Answer you will never hear:

I told you my name. This may seem strange or unfair, perhaps even a sign of bad faith, but it isn't negotiable. Don't stand there and pretend you never wished or pretended you had another name for yourself. I'm not saying a name of another gender, just in general. Wanting to change my name isn't proof of how insane I am. You have the right to ask questions, and I won't hold that against you. It is my right not to tell you; of course I don't expect you to show me the courtesy of accepting that. You are not the first person I'm having this discussion with. Not even close to being in the first fifty. I told most of the first hundred and got devastating consequences as a result. My good faith has been betrayed and will only be reconciled if we wind up knowing each other for a substantial period of time and my name comes up for totally separate reasons, for example if we ever travel across a border together. Until then ... know that my name is Mat(t), call me by that name and don't expect too much kindness out of this jaded, perceived asshole. My only hope is that I will have managed to someday have you ask yourself some if not all of the questions I've asked myself. But in the meantime, asking me instead is no longer an option.

Trials of Education

Jim Lemoire

Stigmatized, Tolerated
Mixed Media Photography, 2001

Questioning the notion of encouraging tolerance as a means of promoting equity, the link between the oppression of stigmatization and the oppression of being simply tolerated, rather than accepted, is explored.

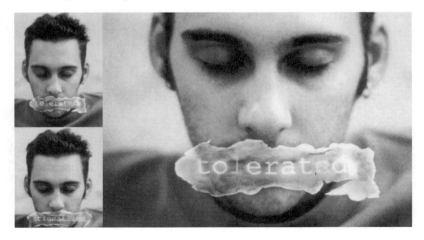

Front and Back

Photography, 2001

The experience of students whose sexual or gender identities have been acknowledged or assumed, and how educators and other students often stigmatize them. The superimposed view from the front and back of the class emphasizes what is seen or not seen, known or not known, shared or not shared due to feelings of isolation.

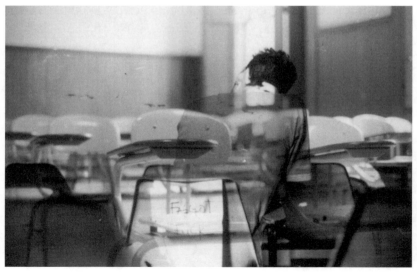

What your class means to her
Mixed Media Photography, 2001

Identity and experiences of queer adolescents within Canada's educational system. Based on a letter from a First Nations lesbian to me in February 2001, it explores the contrast between the purpose  of a classroom and the reality of attending classes in homophobic and heterosexist environments and the division between the chairs students occupy and the perception of an educator's experience, encouraging a dialogue regarding environments that are conducive to learning.

Stolen Identity
Mixed Media Photography, 2001

The changing perception of being two-spirit within First Nations communities since colonialization, the cultural assimilation and stigmatization of being two-spirit since the intrusion of colonialism and the problem of how Western homophobic perceptions are deeply embedded and adopted within some First Nations communities today.

Anxiety

Mixed Media Photography, 2001

The implications of being stigmatized on physical health — the experience of having a heart rate of 186 is the reality of a queer individual who suffers from panic attacks related to significant levels of anxiety stemming from 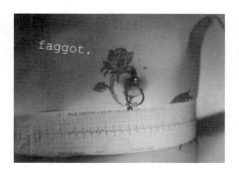 stigmatization — and the unique contrast between self-embraced notions of difference, as implied by the tattoos and piercings, and imposed notions of difference, as implied by the heart rate.

Nine cuts into the cat's life, but she's still kicking

Suzy Yim

After writing this piece, I sit back, puzzled, distraught, even amazed at some of the things that have happened. It still hurts me to look back at the events that I have mentioned below, and I think that I will forever have unanswered questions. Fortunately, things have changed for the better. I can proudly say that I survived the stumble out of the closet, the touch of the paternal fist and the sting of the homophobe's blade. I am a twenty-year-old, fully independent woman. I am queer, and I am not ashamed!

I would like to thank my friend Anu. You picked me up when no one else could. I owe you my life, for I don't know what would have happened if you hadn't been there for me. Amy, I never knew that I could love someone as much as I love you. Thank you for loving me as much as I love you and for showing me the many colors of intimacy. Each day is a beautiful day because I wake up beside you. To my sister, you have been a constant support to me and I am glad that you now *know the truth. When I write about the "family," you are excluded from the group of domineering sadists I previously lived with. Your continued love has given me hope that when I finally do come out to the family, they may still love me as you still love me. I would also like to send my gratitude to Brad, Linda, Mary and everyone else who told me that it was okay to be me. Thank you all for loving me.*

I joined T.E.A.C.H. because I didn't know if life was worth living. I hope my story will show you insight into how powerful the words and actions of others can be.

How hard is it to be a body without presence, a soul without an identity? How hard is it to fear oneself so much that all you can do is run away? How long can you run before you collapse from exhaustion ... bleeding, sweating, crying on the cold pavement? I started running when I was six, and it wasn't until I was eighteen that someone told me I didn't need to run anymore.

Running ...

Alone: to be apart from other persons or things; solitary.

Synonyms: abandoned, deserted, desolate, detached, forsaken, isolated, lonesome, separate, solitary, unconnected.

A study by behavioral psychologist Harry Harlow showed that, left in isolation, an animal will turn to self-mutilation. What exactly is isolation? In Harlow's experiments, it was being apart from others, but have you ever noticed that you could be surrounded by people, yet at the same time be completely alone? What a paradox. Did you know that neglect and emotional abuse could be more damaging than physical abuse? Lucky girl I am to have experienced all three.

Life was tough growing up. I had the necessities for my body to survive, but my life was devoid of essence. Who would have thought that in a family of five, I would be so alone? My parents worked hard, they still do, and that necessity to constantly work deprived me of their presence. Both my brother and sister are much older and never wanted to spend time with me because I was too young to do anything cool. I have no other family in Canada, and my parents didn't trust me with strangers. There was me, and there was the world, and it seemed that no bridge united the two. I was alone. Always alone. Oh God, I hated being alone! I felt unwanted. Unloved. No one knew who I was and no one cared, not even me.

As a child I was taken to church, though I think "forced" would probably be a better word. Every Sunday, after the tedious task of trying to get me in the car so we could leave, I would sit in Bible study and learn about the word of God. "God is great," they would say, "his words are the words that you should live by." Many of the kids sat and nodded, "Um-hmm, oh yes." But I had questions. When I was about eight years old, my Bible study leader told the class that homosexuality was wrong. I didn't understand what homosexuality was; in fact, I didn't even know what it meant to be sexual. All I knew was that this was a very bad thing, but no one really told me why. I wondered, but was too afraid to ask.

Life went on. I hated elementary school. The boys were mean and would call me names and hit me because I was different. When I was ten years old I was 5-foot-6 and 180 pounds. That, combined with the fact that I was a racial minority in a 90 percent white school, made me their prime target. I would tell the teacher and the principal that I was being harassed, but they didn't do anything to help. Nothing changed. For three years I endured their hate, but I never understood why they hated and hurt me so much. I would usually just sit and take it, but one day I got sick of it, stuck my foot out, and tripped the source of my misery. He got really upset and started punching me in the face. We were caught and taken to the principal's office. My principal told me I had an aggression problem and suspended me from the class ski trip that was to take place that week. No one seemed to care that my life was miserable, that all I wanted to do was survive. I hated my life. Hated it. I hated being home because I was always alone, but I hated being at school even more. Was there no relief? Who would have thought that a ten-year-old would understand the concept of suicide?

Running ...

Hide: to cover up; to shut off from sight; to keep secret.
Synonyms: camouflage, conceal, disguise, withhold.

As I grew older, I learned new things and became more independent. I was sick of being home alone. My need to live life my way clashed with my family's need to have utter and total control over me. I rebelled. Unfortunately for me, both my father and brother are firm believers in discipline. If a child rebels, then that child should be punished, and so I was. Over and over again. I hated it when they hit me. I felt so angered, so saddened, so worthless, so unloved. How could you hit your own child, your own sister? I would yell in retaliation, but that did me no good because they would just yell louder. The screaming never stopped. Every day there would be a fight. I just wanted to run away, but I couldn't, so instead I hid from them. Hiding ... it seems to have been my perpetual state of being.

If I did have a conversation with my family, it usually consisted of their listing the things wrong with me and telling me what I should or should not do. "You're a spoiled brat." "I don't understand why Mommy and Daddy haven't kicked you out of the house yet." "Stop crying, no one is listening." "No one cares, Suzy." "You look so stupid with that hairdo." "You're too fat; lose some weight." "Study more, you can never study too much." "Homosexuality is wrong." More than once they mentioned how bad it was to be queer. They said that it was not a correct and honorable way to live, that it was full of sin, shame and disgrace. Goodness, why were they telling me this? I was more worried about being too fat!

Running ...

Illusion: an appearance or feeling that misleads because it is not real; a false impression or perception.

Synonyms: deception, delusion, error, fallacy, figment, misconception.

High school was much better. On the first day of school in grade nine, I told myself that things were going to change. I decided that I wasn't going to be the victim anymore, I was going to make a difference, and I was going to be known to the whole school. It worked. I had lots of friends and was very successful, winning all kinds of academic and athletic awards. My teachers thought I was the pick of the litter. "Look at her," the kids would say, "she's the president and she's won this and that...." Apparently, I was the envy and pride of the student population. On the outside, I had the perfect life; I was pure gold. But there was a profound emptiness and piercing pain that I was too afraid to understand.

Running ...

Queer: not usual or normal; mentally unbalanced; slang for homosexual; one of abnormal sexuality.

Synonyms: fag, dyke, cocksucker, carpet-muncher, muff-diver, fence-sitter, nymphomaniac, cross-dresser.

At school I got respect. No one hurt me or made fun of me. They made fun of other kids, the ones who looked like fags and queers. I would hear it down the halls, "Don't look at me, you ugly faggot!" I didn't do anything about it. Maybe I should have, but what did I care? They probably really were anyway. Sometimes when I was really angry at someone, I would call them a faggot. To me, that was the deepest insult. Nobody wants to be a queer. The boys are such pansies and the girls are so butch that you can't even tell that they're girls. Boy, was I glad I wasn't one of them. I was a girl who liked boys. I had crushes on them all the time, so that meant I couldn't possibly be one of those queers that everyone was yelling about. Sure I had thoughts about other girls sometimes, but I was young ... all youngsters have thoughts about the same sex; it's part of growing up. I mean, I knew that girls were hot, but that didn't mean I was a dyke — no way. It just meant I was envious of girls who were prettier than me. Maybe these thoughts were provoked because I was beginning to think about sex and girls are highly sexualized. I don't know. Whatever the reason, I knew I was straight and that was what was important. Well, that's what I told myself, and I was quite content believing it. I can't believe how homophobic I was.

Running ...

Come out: to declare oneself in some way; slang for declaring one's sexual orientation.

Synonyms: open up, be truthful about oneself.

Things were great until my last year of high school. Until then I had managed to survive the wrath of my family and push away all those silly thoughts about girls. Then my world began to crumble and a chain of events nearly destroyed me. In the second week of school, I tore my Achilles tendon playing basketball and couldn't walk for two months. This depressed me because I was very active and sports were my love and my stress release. It was my last year of high school and I had to spend it on the sidelines. I went to the first home game and it hurt to watch them play. I wanted to be there with them, with all my friends. Then, during this time of need, my best friend decided to stop being friends with me. I'm still a little puzzled about what happened to end our relationship, but something did. Things were getting bad at home, too; there was constant fighting and the intensity was escalating. I was stressed out and depressed. My friend Anu empathized with my injury and saw how the sudden and unexplained loss of my best friend caused me great distress. She would talk to me and say, "It will be okay." Anu and I became very good friends that year. We got to know each other on more intimate levels, and I soon came to realize what a wonderful and genuine friend she was.

One day, when I checked my e-mail, I saw that she had sent something to me. I opened it and it contained a link to a website that was to predict my future love. Normally I would have deleted the e-mail, but I thought, "What the heck, why not?" The form asked me all these questions like my name, my birthday, who my first crush was, etc. One question asked if I was attracted to members of the same sex. I didn't really think about this question and just instinctively clicked "yes." When I clicked "done," to my surprise and horror, a window popped up stating that my answers were sent to Anu. It then showed me what I had written. It said my name, my birthday, so on and so forth, but then it said those scary, scary words: "She is bisexual." I freaked out. I didn't know what to do! What if Anu thought I was bisexual?! My fear turned to rage and I sent her a very nasty and vulgar e-mail. I swore at her, saying she was a bad friend and that she shouldn't pry into people's business. I was so afraid and I couldn't even be bothered to think about why.

When Anu called later that night I didn't want to talk, but felt that I had to convince her I was straight. I kept on saying that the answers were all wrong and that the only reason I was mad at her was because she tricked me. After a long conversation, I thought that for sure Anu didn't believe I was queer. Just to make sure, I asked her what she learned from our conversation, and she replied, "If I want to know something, I should just ask you in person and not try to trick you into answering." Good, I thought, she thinks I'm straight. Then just to make sure, I asked her, "Did you learn anything else?" and to my horror she said, "Yeah, I think I learned a little more about you."

It was at that point that I completely lost it. She thinks I'm bisexual. Oh my God, I am bisexual! I couldn't talk, I couldn't even breathe! A million thoughts were flying through my brain and they were all memories of how I was attracted to girls and how I wanted to kiss them and hold them, how some made my heart pulse faster and my stomach flutter. I remembered the week before when I saw *Charlie's Angels* and I said to a friend: "Lucy Liu is hot!" I remembered how curious and interested I was in learning who all the queer girls were and how they made me nervous. I even had a memory of when I was six years old and was especially drawn to a female classmate. I protested this revelation. There was no way that I was queer. No way! Oh God, what is my family going to say? They'll love me even less than they already do! I can't afford that. I'm trying to give them reasons to love me! I must hide this. I must hide this from everyone. This isn't true. This isn't true.

I was in denial. Pure denial. I was desperate for any excuse that would cover this mess up, anything. Anu talked to me for a long while after about my epiphany, telling me that it was okay, that I didn't have anything to be ashamed of. I wasn't listening to her because I was too busy trying to convince myself that I was straight. I didn't succeed.

Things were a mess. I was stressed and detached from the world. I had a hard time looking at Anu and acting normally. I felt like everyone who saw me could see that I was abnormal. I was so self-conscious that I grew my hair long and wore girly clothes so I didn't look like a dyke. No matter how hard I tried to be straight, I knew I wasn't. Then it happened; I developed feelings for my friend, Jess.

Running ...

Attraction: to be drawn to something or someone.

Synonyms: allurement, enticement, magnetism.

Jess and I played on the badminton team, and in that last year of high school we were partners for girls' doubles. I had recovered from my injury, and although I was not supposed to play sports, I decided to hit the courts. Jess and I practiced every night from 3:15 to near 6:00. We were good pals.

One day, a friend told me that Jess was very upset. I hadn't seen her yet that morning, so I went in search of her to find out what was wrong. She looked very dismal, and when I asked her what happened, she started to cry, so I held her in my arms. She told me that the night before a stranger was watching her from the bathroom window while she was taking a shower. The window was on one of the walls of the shower and he had reached his arm through the window to grab her. Fortunately, she noticed in time and ran to call her brother, who then called the police. She wasn't dealing with it very well. She said that she didn't trust anyone and that she couldn't be left alone anymore because she was so scared that someone might hurt her or that the man would come back. I told her that I would stay with her every day until her brother got home from university so that she would never be alone. And I did.

Every night after practice, I went to her house. I usually stayed very late, even after her brother got home, frequently until 10:00 p.m. For months I did this, and over time, feelings began to grow. I tried to repress them, but I couldn't. I wanted to tell her because part of me thought it was mutual. We did things that many friends wouldn't do, like buy each other spontaneous gifts and make crafty presents for each other. At our school dance we even danced together, grinding and everything. Maybe, just maybe, she felt the same way. I was afraid to tell her that I liked her, so I thought that maybe I would tell her about my sexual orientation first. I was also too afraid to do that, but one day after weeks of contemplation, I told her. To my surprise, she said she knew! Great! I thought to myself. That means that she doesn't mind that I like girls, that she won't judge me. I was very happy, but I decided to leave it at that, not mentioning my feelings for her.

I spent a lot of time wondering how she felt about me. I hoped that she liked me — after all, why would she make me so many gifts and dance sexually with me if she suspected I was queer all along? I still didn't have the guts to ask her for fear of her response. I had other things to think about too; we did very well in girls' doubles for badminton and made it to the Ontario finals. I told myself that I would let her know after the competition, so that if she didn't want to hang around me she wouldn't have to because our badminton season would be over. We did very well in the tournament, coming home with the silver medal. I was happy, but

I knew that I had to let her know soon or I would burst.

Soon after we came back to Toronto, I decided that enough was enough and that I would tell her. I said that I needed to talk and so we went over to her house like we always did. She sat down on the kitchen chair and I stood up, too nervous to sit. She asked me what I wanted to talk about, and my palms began to sweat. I looked at her, then looked away. Was I really going to do this? Oh God. Yes, I have to. I looked back at her and said shakingly, "I think I have feelings for you." She looked at me confused and with a disgusted look on her face. "In that way?" she asked. I nodded. "That's so icky!" That's so icky. That was her response to what I had waited months to tell her. I was getting even more nervous. "Please, I don't want this to ruin our friendship." She looked up at me and merely said, "I can't be friends with you anymore."

Running ...

Anguish: agonizing physical or mental distress.

Synonyms: agony, distress, grief, pang, torment, torture.

I left Jess' house that night with tears rolling down my face. How could this be? I spent months at her house, making sure that she was never alone, comforting her about her fears. I was always there for her, but in my time of complete vulnerability, she turned her back on me, forgetting our friendship and all that I had done to make her life easier. How could she be so cold? Is being who I am such a bad thing?

My whole world had collapsed. I decided that I couldn't tell anyone anymore. I would just hide it for the rest of my life. I would marry a man and push this away forever ... if that was how she reacted, how would my parents react? Oh God, I can't be this. I don't want to be this. I hate being this!

I cried at Anu's house as she tried to comfort me. I felt so much pain that I could feel nothing at all. I was numb. I hated myself so much that nothing mattered. I didn't care about anything I had achieved. I didn't care about the good friends I had. I didn't care about anything.

My soul hurt so much that I felt my body needed to feel pain too. The next day I took a blade and put nine slashes across my left wrist. I cut the same spots repeatedly, digging into the flesh. Blood dripped everywhere, but I didn't care. I didn't even feel it because my heart hurt so much more than any physical pain could. I just kept thinking that I would never be loved and that all I wanted was to know that I was loved, by anyone. I didn't feel my family loved me, and hell, if they found out they would really hate me. My best friend had turned on me earlier that year, and now Jess. To my mind, I had nothing. I was empty and depressed.

Although I didn't know it then, I had so much. I had Anu. Anu wiped up the blood. She talked to me every day, always asking me how I felt and if I was doing better. She was so good to me. She carried me to a better, safer place. I thank her for my life.

But even while receiving her constant support, I needed more. I still needed to talk, so I confided in elders I trusted. My English teacher at the time noticed my sudden emotional collapse and offered to help. I was hesitant at first, but her soft voice and the look of genuine concern won me over. We talked frequently, and that helped more than I thought it could. Soon I gained more confidence and spoke to my vice principal, a mentor and friend to me, who was also concerned with my unusual behavior. She too acted as a tremendous support, always leaving her door open for me to come in and pour my heart out. I told my other very good friend, Brad, and he was there for me too. They all told me that I was still a beautiful and accomplished woman, that I had nothing to be ashamed of. Over time, I began to believe them. I began to accept myself. I still wasn't happy with who I was, but I didn't hate it as much. I thought that if they could still love me, maybe I could love myself too.

Running ...

Abuse: to mistreat.

Synonyms: betray, desecrate, dishonor, maltreat, defame.

While things were cooling down with my sense of who I was, things began to heat up at home. I went out against my parents' wishes. My father was very displeased that I was not focused and always wanted to be with my friends. I couldn't explain that I needed to talk to Anu, to see her so she could make things better for me. He and my mother thought I was being "deviant" and wanted me to study.

Then one day my father burst. I opened the door to leave but he blocked my way. I pushed his arm out of the way, and the next thing I knew he had thrown me into the wall, wrapped his hands around my neck and was strangling me. I was in shock. He threw me onto the ground and sat on my torso, his hands even firmer around my neck. I couldn't breathe. I couldn't believe he was doing this! I was used to the burn from his belt, the sting from the wooden spatulas I used to cook dinner and the various other objects that were in his reach, but this was a whole new level. My mother was crying and trying to pull my father off me. When I finally got his hands off my neck, he began slapping and punching me. Noticing that he had no belt on, my father instead hit me across the head, face and body with a shoe. I kicked him off me, but that just made him more furious. Brad had come to pick me up and witnessed what was going on. He came running after my father, screaming at him to stop. My dad chased Brad, but fortunately Brad escaped. Then my father returned to finish me.

I had never fought back, never done more than crawl into the fetal position as a child or push him off as I got older. I was disciplined to take my beating. This time I reached the end of my tolerance; I couldn't take anymore. I became very angry. I threw him off me and every time he came to hit me more, I resisted even more. I held his arms to prevent him from punching me and I leaned my body forward to minimize his kicking range. The fight went on forever. Finally I managed to run out the door. It was near midnight and I was outside. I started to scream, "Come hit me Abba! Come hit me out here where everyone can see you!" My mother ran after me, begging me to stay.

I stood on the front lawn as she cried while kneeling on the grass, holding my pants. There was a lot of yelling and screaming and the neighbors told me to shut up and respect the peace of those who wished to sleep. Then Brad's mother phoned and told my father that she had called the cops. My father yelled and swore at her then hung up. He was angry, but the phone call did something — it calmed him down. He didn't come outside to hit me or drag me back in the house. He didn't come outside at all. After the call he sat quietly at the kitchen table and held his face in his hands. I could see him through the open door. I wasn't sure what he was thinking. A part of me wondered if he was regretting that he had hurt me so viciously. I wondered if he was sorry that he hit me or sorry that he got caught. Shortly after that the cops came to settle the disturbance.

From that day on, I knew that I had to hide my identity from my family. It hurt to think that I would live a lie, but I was afraid. I'm still afraid. If Jess reacted the way she did, then I couldn't imagine how my family would react. I still think about how they would tell me that homosexuality was wrong. And how bad it was to be queer. "Nothing can justify such an impure life." I sometimes worry why they brought it up to begin with, why they continue to mention it. Did they suspect me before I even knew what the words meant? Did they want to take all precautions to prevent me from "turning" that way? Are they testing me to see if I am queer? I still don't know. All I knew was that Jess wouldn't talk to me anymore, and I didn't want the same thing to happen with my family.

Running ...

Heal: to repair by natural process.

Synonyms: amend, cure, remedy, restore, settle, soothe.

That summer I went to Korea to spend some quality time with my sister, who had left Canada three years prior. I missed her dreadfully. She was the one person in my family I could talk to about at least most things, the one person who would stand up for me when I fought with my family. The trip was unexpected and sudden. I thought it was a peace offering of some sort, a way to say I'm sorry for hurting you, so here's a nice birthday present. My father later informed me that he sent me to get some discipline from my sister and the extended family. Fortunately, though, my sister doesn't side with my father. She just told me that he wanted me to calm down a bit and left it at that. Still, though, I would have preferred if he just pretended that he sent me there because he wanted me to have a good time.

I loved going to Korea. I loved seeing my sister and extended family. I also loved the country's beautiful balance between luscious landscapes and busy city streets. Even though I was having a blast, I couldn't stop thinking about what happened with Jess. I couldn't stop thinking about how we were before I told her, how close we were and why she acted the way she did, so intimately. Part of me believed and still believes that she was having trouble dealing with her sexuality and thus ran away from me, the one who forced her to question it. Of course, I have no proof of this, but it's a working theory. The thoughts filled my mind frequently and with no one to talk to about it, it was hard.

The thing that probably bothered me the most was when my sister saw my cut wrist. She was very upset and asked me what was wrong, what had made me do such a horrible thing. I then got even more upset because I couldn't tell her. I wanted so much to tell her that I had just had the worst year of my life, that I was hurt more than I ever thought I could be, so much that I wanted to die. But I couldn't. I couldn't tell her that I was dealing with my sexuality, that I was queer. I was just too afraid. So afraid. She was the one person in my family I could have a pleasant conversation with, and there was no way I was going to risk losing that. No way. All I told her was that something bad happened and I didn't deal with it well. She was not satisfied with my answer, but said that she would wait until the day I could tell her. For the most part, I had an enjoyable trip that helped take the stress off my mind.

Freedom ...

A right or a privilege, exemption from obligation.

Synonyms: unrestricted, emancipation, independence, liberation, release.

The real turnaround for me was going to university. I hadn't signed up to live in residence for first year, but after a couple weeks of school it was looking very tempting. The arrival of my scholarship and a large monetary gift from my sister provided me with a chance to apply. I was very lucky that a girl wanted to move out that same weekend and I got a spot immediately. My life changed at that very moment. When I received the room, I closed the door, sprawled across the bed, shut my eyes and smiled. I no longer had to live with control freaks. I no longer had to worry about being hit or yelled at. I didn't even have to worry about getting up early for school! This was my newfound sanctuary, and I was on cloud nine. My parents couldn't stop me either because they weren't paying for a dime of my education and so had nothing to threaten me with. For once, I was in control.

Immediately I wanted to start looking for queer-positive

things. But I was very hesitant at first and kept my identity quite sealed. I met so many wonderful, open-minded, nonjudgmental people, but still chose not to tell them. I was still nervous. My first move was small, but a huge leap for me. I put a positive sticker up on my dorm door. My door was already decorated to the max with Winnie the Pooh and other cute, colorful pictures, so the little rainbow sticker was nearly unnoticeable. Still, the act of putting it up made my heart thump faster and my palms sweat. Immediately after I put the sticker up, I shut the door to direct attention away from me. Whew.

In the next few weeks, I made friends with many people who remain close and dear to my heart. I was happy, social and enjoying every drop of my freedom. I can't tell you how good it felt. I went out every weekend. I signed up for LGBTOUT, the University of Toronto's queer student group, and was regularly informed of all the queer events around the campus area. I went to many of them and even went on dates with girls. I told myself that I wouldn't try to get into a relationship because I was worried I would get hurt again. All I wanted to was to meet people and have some fun. Then it happened again, but this time, it was good.

Love ...

A passionate affection for another person.
Synonyms: Amy.

Amy and I met through a mutual friend. We lived in the same residence and had a class together. When I first met Amy, I thought she was pretty kooky, and I had no idea of the relationship that was to follow. Amy and I were very good friends right from the beginning. We spent many hours just talking about anything and everything. One day, we were talking about males we thought were attractive and she said, "Sometimes I like looking at girls' butts." I was taken aback and became nervous again. I mustered my courage and decided to come out to her. I told her that I was bisexual. She was the first friend I verbally came out to, and I was shaking inside. To my delight, she wasn't appalled or disgusted; in fact, she was questioning her own sexuality. We talked for days. We formed a very strong and special relationship.

Soon it was clear that our connection was more than just friendship. A month and a half after we first met, we were dating: A month and a half after that, we moved in together. We decided that since we were always together anyway, we might as well share a room and save some money. It was a big step, but we took it confidently.

Relief ...

The sensation following the easing or lifting of discomfort or stress.

Synonyms: alleviation, ease, softening.

That February, my sister came to Canada. She was on vacation and wanted to see the family. She had serious conversations with me about university and experimentation and sex. Basically she said no, no, no! The conversation about sexual orientation was frequent and we argued a lot. We obviously had different opinions on why people were queer. She saw it more as experimentation and the last resort of not being able to find companions of the opposite sex. I challenged her and told her my arguments. She was open to new understanding, but still held on to many of her initial views. It was clear that something was up, but we didn't go any deeper into the conversations. A couple of weeks later, she left for Korea again.

The talks with her bothered me. I was worried. Why was she talking about it so much? Why did her views have to be so disappointing? I was upset. Each time we phoned and e-mailed, she asked me if I wanted to tell her anything new. I would hesitate, then say no. Then one day, it all came out.

I had called her to see how she was doing, and somehow the conversation turned toward me. She said she knew, that I shouldn't hide it from her anymore. I told her that I knew she knew, and I began to cry. I couldn't even explain my emotions. I was just scared. She told me that it was okay, that she still loved me as much as she ever did, but that she wanted me to be celibate. I told her that wasn't going to happen. Then she asked me if Amy and I were a couple. I said yes through a tear-cracked voice. We talked about it, and it was such an enormous relief. I told her why I cut my wrists, how alone I felt, that I couldn't tell the rest of the family and that she couldn't either. I was relieved, and although we had many disagreements still, it felt so good.

I ended the conversation with red eyes, a headache and a sense of both relief and distress. I was relieved she knew, but distressed at our very different opinions. I told Amy about it and she made me feel better, just like she always does. Over time, my sister began to understand me more and showed immense support.

Things are even better between us than they were before because there is nothing I am hiding from her now. I love that I can share such an inmate part of my life with someone in my family. I love that she likes Amy and that Amy likes her too. Maybe one day I will be able to tell the rest of my family.

Queer ...

An umbrella term used to incorporate all who are not straight or do not wish to be classified by their sexual orientation; a person who may love another of the same sex.

Synonyms: me.

My life has changed so much in the last three years. My troublesome last year of high school taught me to be strong in tough situations, to be proud of who I am and to be aware of my own prejudices. I am much more sensitive to the hardships of others and make it a point to prevent oppression as best I can; thus I have joined organizations such as T.E.A.C.H. Who would have thought that I, an ex-homophobe, would be writing about the struggles I faced about my sexuality?

I'm not running anymore.

✦✦✦

a/li(f)ve to tell

njeri-damali (campbell)

My mere existence in the academic world challenges colonialism. The fact that i write like this, sing like this, breathe like this or breathe at all goes against a larger colonial project bent on my erasure. Is this a little too harsh? Maybe it is. Maybe i'm overreacting, but i don't think so. The tears tell me otherwise.

Telling our own stories can help us (the tellers and the listeners) recreate our understandings of who we are in the world. i am able to write like this because of the path laid out for me by other women (bell hooks, Audre Lorde, Yvonne Campbell, T.J. Bryan aka Tenacious) who continue to tell their stories against the grain, and in the process contribute to our collective emancipation.

July 15

dear mom,

it's getting darker, and i'm still at work, thinking about what i'm doing in my academic career, wondering how to really answer the question that you ask me all the time, "what about your future?" i thought i'd take this opportunity to tell you a little about where i am in the world these days, and what my work is all about.

you know that i studied political science and sociology at York. i graduated with honors, then took a year off to start my position at the Ontario Young People's Alliance. during that year, i applied for a variety of graduate programs and was invited to study education at York in their Language, Culture, and Teaching program. this continues to be a huge challenge for me, because as i progress in my studies, i realize that the work that i do is quite intense and extremely important to me.

when i was younger, being "self-conscious" was a bad thing. it meant, and often felt, as if the world were looking angrily over my shoulder, breathing down my neck, judging me. i've chosen to dodge that trigger, and think of myself as self-reflexive. this means that i operate with the assumption that nothing that i write or that i produce or that i research will ever be disconnected from me. this, by extension, now means that i start from i. i declare that my place in the world is impacted by the matrices of my identity. i am young, Black, queer, middle classed, diasporic, university educated, able bodied, sex positive, natural haired, dark skinned, heterosexy, and, and, and ... i understand the world in this way. the stories that i search for and the stories that i seek will always be anchored by this reality; i am driven by this. "it" — the work that i produce — becomes me.

i have chosen to turn my critical gaze toward a system (the school system) that i struggled in and was rewarded by. you and dad saw the side of school that others did. you saw my report cards, which were usually pretty good. you saw me go to summer school and then be employed at summer school. you witnessed the awards, the speeches, the special attention and the scholarships. many others did too: our fellow church families, our neighbors and family friends, even some of my own teachers. you saw all this and celebrated it with me, and for that i thank you.

but there was so much more than that. i remember my grade three teacher, who had bright red hair and pale white skin; she seemed so tall back then. she was from Ireland, i think. anyway, she had a program called student of the month. in this program, one student was chosen each month, based on something special they did or their marks. the winning student each month would get their name put up on the board, along with a photograph. gold and red stars would be festooned around their face, and they would also get a nice certificate.

i wanted, more than anything, to be student of the month. it was the last full month of school — May, my birth month — and some of my classmates had told me that i would probably be chosen. i kept my hopes up ... the first few days of May passed by, and no student was chosen! "why?" i wondered. i thought maybe she had stopped early this year, or maybe she was still deciding. one whole week passed by, and another, and another ... no choice was made. someone asked her one day in class, "mi-iss?" the student said, with her hand up high, "who's the student of the month?" the class fell silent, eager to hear her response. "Njeri Campbell," our teacher responded simply and returned to her work.

i was devastated. i had been chosen student of the month? and she waited three weeks to put it up on the board? why didn't she celebrate me like the others?

a few days after, school was dismissed for the holidays, and i, embarrassed, left the class, sadder than ever. i would have preferred not being chosen over this sorry state of affairs.

this wasn't the first such event and was definitely not the last. i came up against school as an institution in so many ways. often when i made complaints, or explained my situations, you and dad told me not to be so sensitive; the authority figures at the school told me that nothing could be done.

that was difficult to deal with, and as a result i developed a very violent anger toward my teachers, which resulted in many conflicts. when i switched schools and i went to St. Andrew's French immersion program, things got even worse. i had decided to shift my identity and symbolized that shift by changing the pronunciation of my name. "Na-je-raye" i told people to call me, and Na-je-raye i became. Na-je-raye was funny, the new girl in class, not so good in French but very good in English. Na-je-raye was rich. although she lived in a lower-income, working-class part of the city, she told people that her family was rich, that she had a butler and many limousines.

at first, people believed her, and many of the students around her wanted to be her friend. but, little by little, the other girls at school found her out. one day after class they cornered her in the yard.

i remember that day very well.

the ringleader came up to me and said: "we know that you're a liar. why do you say all this stuff that's not true?" i pretended i didn't know what she was talking about. i felt my lunch coming back up my throat and my knees buckling. i continued to shiver in fear and the girls closed in on me and proceeded to tell me every lie i had ever told them, from the most innocent to the most elaborate of them all. i was very embarrassed, and finally i gave in and told them that they were right. immediately after that confession, one girl stepped up from the group and said that they had all decided to forgive me, as long as i vowed never to lie again. i promised them all that i wouldn't, and that i would do my best to undo the wrongs i had done.

i walked home that evening alone, but free. i felt, for the first time, that a group of girls, a group of girls i had tried so hard to befriend, saw me for who i was and chose to love the truth of me. i didn't have to pretend anymore.

that group of girls became my clique, and i, the photographer of the elementary unit, became their herstorian. remember that 110 camera i won at the church bazaar? with that camera, i captured so many moments at school. i tried out for the volleyball and basketball teams, but i didn't make it. i tried out for the cross-country team and didn't make the quarter finals, but i got to go to the track meet and (of course) take pictures of all the cool athletes. the only success i had was in W5H, the team of smart students who battled against other schools, asking each other skill-testing questions. we were a pretty good team, and i had a lot of fun, although it was scary and the boys on the team were aggressive and sometimes downright mean.

the teachers were okay, except when my French-immersion teacher threw chalk at me and bruised my collarbone, and when they always sat me in the back row of the class, or when i was denied access to elective courses or special events at school.

the other students knew what was happening, but they remained quiet, and i remained alone, trying to be healthy, trying to have friends and trying to be cool.

luckily, throughout all this drama, there was a church community of elders who, in their own ways, supported my growth and development. they liked me and supported my accomplishments. i especially liked the families who chose not to put me in competition with their children by telling them that they should be more like me.

finally grade eight came, and thanks to you and dad fighting for me, i was placed in the advanced stream. i could go on to university after high school.

high school was more of the same in some ways, but a little bit harder. i found the school work quite easy (i still have my notes and stuff) and the teachers seemed pretty happy to have me there. for most of grade nine, i hung around with some friends from elementary school, and i made friends with the gifted teacher, the guidance counselor, and my math teacher. i had those huge, black, owl-like glasses that were crooked, and i didn't really think i was particularly attractive. people laughed at me and called me ugly a lot. i really wanted to have my hair braided with extensions.

i got good marks, joined the student council, and created a new position there. i quickly became known as i started creating space for myself to speak on the morning announcements (people really liked my voice) and contributing to the social activities of the school. grade ten came and went with one of my more intense student/teacher relationships. i challenged my teachers because i was completely fascinated by them. i wanted to know about their lives, what brought them to teaching, what made them an expert. i complained a lot and many of them found me unbearable. i got mad at my history teacher for not teaching about "Natives," my English teacher for making us read Shakespeare, our French teacher for not telling me the truth about "the Algiers" and so much just went completely out of whack.

i am often reminded that this work, the work i did, the work i do, and my dreams are painfully overdue.

i soon became known for my "arrogant" questioning nature and my temper tantrums. in social studies class, when my teacher walked up to my desk and slid all my belongings off of it because i hadn't cleared them away fast enough for my test, i walked out of class and slammed the door so hard that it freaked even me out. i did the same when a teacher gave me a low grade on a project about Egypt when the class decided it was the best project in the class. on both occasions i went straight down to the principal's office, and then to the guidance office, to cry and yell. and it worked.

did you know about any of this?

i'll continue to tell the stories though. for now, that is the only way that my work can breathe. i must tell the stories, starting with my own. for now, that is the only way that my work can bleed. i must tell the stories starting with my own. i have died and been re-born many times. i have lost and loosed and have hovered in the places where there was nothing but silence. the challenge to the colonial comes when i survive and thrive and — as Madonna croons — "hope I live to tell the secret I have learned; till then, it will burn inside of me...."

burning, yes.

grade eleven changed everything.

i began the youth council, started the tv show, started attending many, many leadership conferences, got chosen to represent the school and discovered boys. that's when i permed my hair again and got contact lenses. the school kilt got shorter, and the navy blue tights of my uniform were exchanged for knee-high socks. the lipsticks came in dark raspberry and sometimes ginger, the eyes lined in Bonne Bell's smoky kohl, and i wore Chloë every day.

i was hot. the boys, some girls and some teachers sensed the change in my ways, and attention came like crazy. i was smart, pretty, popular, funny and had a bad temper. i knew my way around the classroom and the school. i knew how to get into and out of things, and i knew what was worth the struggle and what wasn't. the freedom was incredible.

i started to hear rumors about me. the teachers didn't like me, and the students in my grade thought i was a snob. i had two or three friends throughout high school, but i didn't really have the time to give the time of day to anyone. i stopped working in groups for project work because i couldn't meet up with people because of my after-school meetings or my shoots for the tv show i ran. i was fast paced, forward looking, confident seeming, aloof.

i ran for student council president and lost. people laughed at what i have recently been told was the most embarrassing election speech ever. i dressed up as a clown; no one laughed. i felt awful.

grades twelve and thirteen went by with more of the same. things started to calm down and my life shifted away from a school i didn't feel a part of. on some occasions, students and teachers colluded with each other to sabotage my attempts at projects and programming in the school. people were tired of Na-je-raye. in some ways, i was too.

The Dilemmas:
- passion
- fatigue
- fear
- holding my story over others
- playing the game
- the quest for validation

i was happy to leave and enter York, my next playground.

first year was great. i joined a lot of groups, like the Women's Centre, the New Democratic Party, and the Catholic Student Centre (church every day, remember?). my classes were tough, with all the reading and writing and lack of confidence in my writing. i had some great teaching assistants who taught me more about writing in their five-minute post-classroom chats than any of my high-school English teachers did. i was independent.

in second year, i dropped the Catholic Centre and the Women's Centre and started, instead, to meditate. i developed a language about my sexuality as i started meeting other people i could talk to about my attractions to wimmin. my classes became more interesting. i ran for school board trustee in our city, and i kept up a good average. i became president of a campus group, and i joined student government. i also drank my first pint of beer — and enjoyed it.

i took on the name "Na-je-ree," as you named me. it took a while for people to notice the shift and then to honor it, but it came soon enough. it was nice having people call me what you and dad called me at home. it was a release of a self that I had grown impatient with, a coming home, a re:birthing.

then i met Njeri, my first namesake sistah friend. we both changed our names again to the current pronunciation, one that you do not use, "in-jeri." i started to write my name in lower case, and put the "campbell" in parentheses to honor your line, the strachans.

although i enjoyed the freedom i had to write, i detested the reading i had to do, and how most of the readings i read in political science — even the courses that were supposed to be about Black people — were white. that was hard to swallow, and my rage continued to boil as i returned to those high-school days of leaving classes enraged. i met with many of my professors, trying and hoping against hope that they would give me something to trust, and often i was successful. professors, i found, were more willing to "give" than teachers in my previous schools.

i visited some of my profs, got closer with my classmates and wrote some great stuff. sometimes it took a while to get my papers done, but i was creative, fun and resourceful.

the last years of university saw more classes, more friends, more loves and more angst as i wondered what my next steps would be. i put on hold my desire to apply for law school and focused on getting things to think and write about for my graduate studies.

my undergrad ended in a touching graduation ceremony. you and dad attended, and unbeknownst to you, so did my first woman lover. she wore a beautiful red wrap, black sunglasses and gold shoes. she stood up when my name was called. you and dad and auntie joan yelled for me. i smiled at all of you and felt loved and supported.

it was an afternoon of possibility, accomplishment, movement. it prepared me to be here, writing to you about this journey that i've taken and continue to take. it prepared me for the joy and pain of grad school. the excitement of creating and finishing work, the joy of sharing laughter and tears with those who facilitate my learning, the constant breaking of my heart in these dreary hallways, the happiness that will soon shift to something, somewhere else.

i came out, then i moved out, and i had more space than i ever had before.

when i look ahead, i see marie and me studying our Ph.D.s together, loving each other against the grain and against your wishes. i will one day teach students to teach ... challenging them to tell their stories, to tell the tales of their shadowlands like i do. i will encourage them to seek redemption in the hallways, to love hard, to love always.

last month, when we went to see that play about Nelson

Rolihlahla Mandela, and little Nelson was going to leave his village forever, his mother said: "look back!! LOOK BACK!!"

you have said the same thing to me, mom. you challenge me to cherish and remember. and i do. i awaken those memories and i put together the pieces of my own past: little bits like this letter to you, little bits through song and photograph, little bits like tears and glances, little bits.

little bits....

thank you, again, for giving birth to me.

your daughter,
njeri-damali (campbell)

Photo: Babatunde Martins, Summer 2002

The White Picket Fence

Makeda Zook

After spending a year coming out to my school, joining T.E.A.C.H. seemed the obvious choice for me because I knew that homophobia in blatant or subtle forms is hurtful and needs to be addressed and tackled. I don't like the idea of people having to live in fear because of their differences. Over the past year and a half, I have found sharing my story with youth in high schools and group homes to be both an empowering and frightening experience. I have learned that however scary it may be to share personal growth and struggle with strangers, when an audience is hushed and intently focused, they will listen. I welcome the opportunity that T.E.A.C.H. has given me to make a difference in people's lives. People's lives and stories are continually changing and growing. I know my story is far from finished; this is a chapter, one that carries great importance, but a chapter nonetheless.

Before I knew the connotations of the phrase "the white picket fence," I was a child who only knew what my home and family had to offer me: unconditional love. As far as I was concerned, this was all that mattered. As a four-year-old, this was my outlook on life, on my life. With the socialization that most children face came my understanding of the white picket fence and I began to realize that unfortunately the world didn't recognize the love and happiness given to a child by two lovers and partners in life when defining family.

When I was thrust into the world outside my family and my family's friends, I began to realize that I was different because of my family, because most people don't have two moms and most moms aren't lesbians. Reflecting on this, I am not sure that there was a defining moment when I realized that I, not the kids with a mom and a dad, was the one who was different. However my earliest and clearest memory of being completely aware of my difference was in grade three. Father's Day was coming and a wonderful teacher, who was aware that my moms were lesbians, asked who I wanted to make a Father's Day card for. She did not want to leave me out of the activity, but recognized that I might have difficulty because I didn't have a father, only a sperm donor. I racked my seven-year-old brain trying to come up with men I cared about in my life and came up with this: my dead grandfather and my male guinea pig. Tough choice, but in the end I ended up making a card for Chocolate, my guinea pig.

It wasn't until grade four that I remember feeling fearful because my moms were lesbians. It wasn't the kind of fear that my physical well-being was in jeopardy. I was afraid that my new friends would stop being friends with me when or if they found out or came to my house. Over the next few years I became very secretive and went to great lengths to prevent my friends or any other students from finding out about my moms. Little did I know that most people knew and that they talked about it behind my back. Some of the people who knew about my moms were the same people who made homophobic remarks. I was lucky that I was never directly targeted, but homophobia was always there, along with constant reinforcement that being gay was a bad thing. The phrase "that's so gay" was among the most popular insults. The homophobia continued and worsened throughout middle school and I began to feel more than fearful. I felt ashamed, even angry that my family didn't fit into the norm of all that the white picket fence embodied.

I could hardly wait for high school. I wanted a fresh start in a place where no one would know my business. When the time came to choose a high school, I had narrowed it down to two. The one I felt more drawn to for its specialized art programs was my first choice, except that one of my moms worked there, not to mention that she was very out at the school. I felt all that familiar fear again. In the end I made the decision that was right for me, and I chose what I truly wanted over my fears. But this didn't mean that I wasn't still afraid. In fact, for all of grade nine and the beginning of grade ten, I went to great lengths to ignore and disassociate myself from my mom. This choice, however, had an effect at home no matter how much I tried to prevent it. I had always had a good relationship with my mom and because of this I was torn. I didn't want my choice to hurt her but I also wanted to protect myself. To this day I don't know how much I hurt her, but I know that being closeted about my family put a strain on our relationship. It wasn't until midway through grade ten that I began to realize what I was putting myself and my mom through. Finally, with the help of a couple of individuals, I began to feel safe enough to come out to my peers.

The individuals who helped, inspired and influenced me were two people I had met the previous year. One was my favorite teacher, the other was a friend who also had a lesbian mom and led by example. Finally, after all the years of being afraid and keeping it pent up inside me, I began to come out. This meant leaving my fear and inhibitions behind. My actions began to reflect this. I had ignored my mom for about a year before, but now I no longer did. So when people asked questions about her, I answered them truthfully and with ease. My peers received this positively. I started doing this at my school and then slowly expanded to other aspects of my life. The more people I was open with, the more the fear dissolved. I gained confidence in myself and felt more able to express my ideas and opinions. All the fear I held inside had left me feeling tense and had created a barrier between my mom and me. But by opening up it felt as if a huge weight had been lifted from my chest and off our relationship.

Homophobia has been a major part of my life — present from a young age, it has affected me throughout. It is an obstacle I have been struggling to overcome on both a personal and a public level. Like all experiences in my life, it is one I have grown from. Not only did this experience stir my dormant drive to challenge all forms of discrimination, but it also awakened understandings and perspectives on family. Perhaps my most important understanding was how lucky I am to have a loving, happy family, even if we don't fit into the traditional white picket fence definition of what it means to be a family.

The Woman of My Life

Johan Kim

A† T.E.A.C.H. *we all come from different backgrounds and we all have different stories, some cheerful, some sad. We tell our stories to help you realize that we are real people and that we do go through situations that are great or quite difficult. The story I am sharing with you is about how my mum found out I was gay. That became a pivotal moment in my life. This is the story I told at T.E.A.C.H. workshops. I chose to tell it because that moment really made me realize how alone you can feel without the support of family and friends. My story is not a very happy one but despite how things unfolded with my 어머니 (written in Korean that means mother) I had never stopped loving her. I hope you enjoy it.*

"빨리 좀 일어나!!! Hurry, get up!"

With her loud and shrill voice, every morning my mother would shout from the bottom of the stairs to get my brother and me up for school. My mum was a very strict woman. She was fairly big, average height and with a very worn look on her face. She was definitely someone not to argue or fight with. My mum was the sort of person who would be a great dictator — not only did she boss my brother and me around, she also bossed, and I mean bossed, my father to get to work. She was definitely the type of person you'd imagine not to have any emotions whatsoever. But she was the strongest person I knew. I admired her so much. She was the woman of my life.

I come from a very traditional and conservative Korean family. Our family lived together in a townhouse in Scarborough and owned a family restaurant. My parents worked hard at the restaurant while my brother and I went to school and were expected to get nothing less than straight A+s on our report cards. It wasn't easy for us; everyone worked hard to make ends meet. We went to church every Sunday and we sat in the usual front center-row seats with my mum staunchly taking in every word. My parents had dreams of my getting married to a wonderful Korean woman, enjoying my career as a lawyer or a doctor, having two children and living in a big house with a white picket fence. This is what my parents both assumed and expected my future to be like. My mum would often sit with me discussing plans of who I'd become and the grandchildren she'd take care of.

Grade nine, my first year of high school, was a year of new experiences. I made some great friends, joined some sports teams and was even doing well in school. Everything was going well. Except one thing. Rebecca, a good friend of mine, had been talking to our mutual friends about finding out what kind of girls I was interested in. Apparently she had a crush on me but I had no feelings for her. My guy friends kept pushing me to ask her out. They said she was good looking, she was smart, and she had "the body!" whatever that meant. This went on for weeks and things got especially hectic with the prom around the corner. I just couldn't stop thinking about this. Finally I told my guy friends that I was not interested in her at all. One of their responses seemed bizarre to me and actually really got me....

"Are you a faggot or something?"

I had always questioned why didn't I have feelings for women. Why couldn't I just like any of them in the way my guy friends did? One day I got my answer in the sexual education part of my phys ed class. We were watching a video on relationships and there was one scene where two guys were holdings hands and walking. Despite all the jeering from other students, that scene stunned me and right then and there I said to myself, "I'm gay."

I went home that day thinking about it on the bus, eventually missing my stop and having to walk back home, but it felt good to know who I was. That day everything changed. Everything that I had been taught by my parents and my teachers and heard from friends about having a girlfriend, relationships, sex, marriage had changed. I felt liberated, but things started to get more and more difficult because realizing that I was gay meant that I had to hide it. I became extra paranoid around my parents because I knew they would never accept it and I realized that I would not be able to tell them until I moved out of the house. My brother, my friends and my peers used words like faggot, queer and battiman as everyday words. People like them kept on reminding me that being gay was wrong.

As time went by, I felt it all. I felt sad, angry, depressed; I felt I was going to crack! Trying to have a conversation about anything "gay related" with my friends became a laugh session about Ru Paul, being in drag and acting very sissy. I knew many of my friends couldn't help, and turning to my parents was definitely not a choice. These were some turbulent times.

Things eventually looked up after I found a community I could share my experiences with. One day I was fed up and I decided to take a stand on things. I got home from school and ran to the living room, grabbed the yellow pages and hid in my room. Stuck in that small closet of mine, using the dim light shining through the slightly opened door, I looked for anything gay related. Flipping through the pages I came across a group for young people called Lesbian Gay Bisexual Youth of Toronto or LGBYT. Absolutely terrified but determined to meet other people who really understood, I gave the number listed a ring and found that they actually met every Tuesday and Saturday at some place called the 519.

Over the next few days, I was excited and nervous about going to the meetings. Tuesday rolled around and I was a nervous wreck! I came up with some feeble lie for my mum that I was working, which was true — I just wasn't working that day. The subway ride down from Scarborough had my palms sweaty and my legs shaking. It felt like everyone's eyes were on me and that I was wearing a huge sign that said "queer." I reached the 519 Community Centre, a big old sturdy building where the meeting was being held. My nerves were all over the place and I was unable to get myself to go into the building. I just kept walking back and forth on the sidewalk. It was thirty minutes before I forced myself to go into the building and to the auditorium where they held the meetings. And from that moment I had friends. There were many young people who were gay, but also lesbian and bisexual, from different backgrounds, who actually knew what I was going through. I felt that this was my place. I really fit there.

I knew that some people did not accept homosexuality at all. But at this point in my life, I was glad to have found myself friends and a community, as they were essential for me to realize that being gay wasn't bad and it was normal. They helped me remain strong. Marc made me realize this even more. He was one of the first guys at the youth group who introduced himself to me. Since then we have become strong friends. Marc is what some people would call a stereotypical gay person. He loves to dress outrageously, gestures with his limp wrist, plucks his eyebrows and starts every conversation with "Oh my gosh, girl...." Outside the gay community, Marc receives gestures, comments and the occasional shove, but each time he stands tall and continues to be Marc. There is nothing wrong with the way he acts or the way he dresses; Marc is a devoted and good friend to me and countless others.

Over the next few months, Marc and I became close friends, often talking on the phone, hanging out after school. We talked about many things. He told me how he came out to his family, about his dates, and everything I needed to know about the youth group. He was my confidant and I was his.

Still hiding my secret from my school friends and my family, I continued to attend the youth group. I kept lying to my family about my whereabouts on Tuesday nights, and whenever I couldn't make up an excuse to go to the meetings I always talked to Marc on the phone to get caught up. Last Tuesday night was no exception. I had to stay in and study. Marc gave me a ring on the big clunky beige rotary phone that I bought with my own money. It is one of those phones that has an irritating, alarming ring, and worse yet there is static whenever you talk on it. Marc was giving me the lowdown of what was going on at the youth group. Apparently someone broke up!

"Girl, *static* ya know, I'm really glad I am with someone that *static* really likes me."

On the subject of boyfriends Marc had long wondered whom I fancied or what kind of guys I liked. Meanwhile, the phone continued its static melody.

"C'mon, Johan, *static* tell me. Who do you like? Just give me a hint...."

I did have a big crush at that time on one of the facilitators at the group — so after much prodding, I responded.

"I, *static* I sort of like Michael ....*static*...."

I had finally gotten it off my chest that I liked this one person! I was sooo happy. What I didn't know was that my mother was listening on the other line.

"야 네가 호모 야?!?"

My mum screamed at me in Korean something akin to, "Are you a homo?" In Korean there is really no appropriate term for homosexual; just one that queer people have reclaimed, but homo isn't it.

Realizing what had just happened, Marc said,

"Girl, you're on your own...."

Marc's hanging up did not bother me. Under the circumstances, I could understand, and I knew I would be able to call him later.

The static continued for at least twenty seconds with just my mum and me on the line. Hearing the "beep beep beep" that signalled I had not hung up the phone, my mum finally broke the silence.

" 이리 와 "

She asked me to come to her.

My hands began to shake, as did the rest of my body. Fear shot through me like there was no tomorrow. My eyes also glossed over. I didn't want to go upstairs to her room, but did I have a choice? I picked myself up wiping away the tears that ran down my face. I breathed long and hard to calm myself down. Walking up the stairs, passing family portraits of everyone smiling, pictures of happy times, it was ironic to see myself smiling back at me when I was in complete fear. Slowly climbing to the top of the stairs, I was loath to go into her room. It was so quiet you could hear the clock ticking. But if you listened carefully, there was another sound. Getting closer, the sound became clearer and finally, reaching her room, I knew what the sound was. I had never heard this before and I had never expected to hear it ever. The phone was on the floor. My mum was crouched with her face in her hands, crying. The sounds of her sobbing hurt my ears and it made me start to tear up. The one person in my life I never expected to cry was crying.

I honestly did not know what to do. Then, I thought, maybe if

I hugged her things would turn to be just great. It would be exactly like those after-school movies. Everyone hugs at the end and things turn out all right. So, slowly passing the lamp I had given to her as a gift, using the railing at the base of the bed as a support, I edged towards her. I wasn't more than a foot away from her and my arms were open, ready for that big hug. But it wasn't to be.

"가 까이 오지마!"

It was these words that engraved themselves into my memory for the rest of my life. This was the most difficult moment that I have ever experienced. To hear these words from the lips of my mum, "Don't touch me."

I just turned around. I traced back the same path, down the stairs, past the photos of the smiling family and the one of myself still smiling at myself. I reached my room, threw a few clothes into my rucksack and left, knowing that this was a no-going-back situation. I closed the door behind me with that memory still fresh in my head, slightly crying, slightly scared. I called Marc from the nearest payphone and then went to his place. I stayed there for a few weeks.

This experience was a pivotal moment in my life. All of the sudden I was a fourteen-year-old, Korean, gay high-school student who had just left his home and family. I felt really alone and things were rough but I made it through with the support of the friends that I had made at the support group.

This experience began a new life for me. Things were on my terms now and I expected that those who loved me had to come to accept me. Eventually, a few of my old friends came through and understood that Johan was just Johan. They were my true friends.

Even my father turned out to be quite supportive and we became quite close, more than we had ever been before. My brother and my mum had different reactions. My brother unfortunately became almost violent. He was angry because having a "faggot" brother was a hindrance to his own life. For my mum, well, this whole thing was very difficult. She tried really, really hard to talk to me about it and we spent countless days and nights crying, screaming and arguing. She never really accepted it and things were never the same. One day, this strong woman who taught me to hold my head up high went away. The woman of my life left me forever, leaving many questions unanswered and many things unsaid.

It has been around eight years since the day my mum found out I was gay. Now that she is gone, I often think about when we used to sit to discuss plans for my future. But I am left to wonder if my mum would have come to be proud of the person I have become. I am left to wonder if she would have come to be happy for the lover I found. I am left to wonder if she would smile for each and every day that I smile. I wonder about all of this because my mum was the woman in my life.

◆◆◆

Ariel's Story – A Remembrance in Five Parts

Ariel Vente

I've been with the T.E.A.C.H. program for six years in various capacities, from volunteer to staff. I've seen the program grow, morph, change and develop into what it is today. For the past five years, I always told the same story at the workshops. However, during the last year, a very significant event in my life gave me something new to tell. I present to you a new story with some elements from my old story. This is a story of my mother and me growing, morphing, changing and developing.

I knew from my childhood that gay was sin, gay was immoral and gay was white! I lived a double life full of lies and deceit all because I was trying to be true to myself. I didn't know of any other gay Filipino who was like me; there was nobody to look up to, to be my role model. What I did see was that the gay Filipinos I was exposed to were the jokes of the community — the hairdressers, the drag queens, the queer who sold Avon cosmetics; highly feminized and ridiculed for their femininity, they were the butt of people's jokes, the unwitting court jesters. How the hell could that be me? This is what I remember....

✦✦

I remember feeling this tremendous burden, this cloud of guilt that hung over me because of my double life. If my family found out, I was sure my brothers would be disgusted by me, my mother would send me to a priest, my father would disown me and I would be kicked out of my home. *Sin ... immoral ... white....*

A few weeks before my twenty-first birthday, I was on the edge of an emotional breakdown. I felt like I was going to break in half because I was carrying this bag of bricks on my shoulders. *Sin.* My parents sensed this gloominess and despair and needed to know what was wrong with me. *Immoral.* They called me into their room to talk, but I couldn't tell them. All I could do was cry.

My father finally said to me, "I know what's wrong!" But I tearfully told him that he wouldn't understand.

"Yes, I know ..." he insisted.

"No, you don't!"

"Yes, I know ..." he insisted again.

"No, you don't!"

And this went on for a few minutes until he finally said, "It's because you're gay and you just broke up with your boyfriend!"

I was stunned. Even though the second part of that statement was false, the first part was right on the button. Funny how astute some people are! The positive thing was my father didn't disown me but rather was supportive and understanding, and in typical Filipino father-like fashion, his only piece of advice to me was inspired: "Don't do anything stupid!"

But at the moment I was stunned into silence. So was my mother. She was distant and quiet throughout the entire interaction with my father and me. No doubt that she was thinking that her son was a sinner and her son was immoral. I remember her finally declaring, "You just have to marry a good woman!"

I was stunned into silence a second time after that declaration but nonetheless felt relief as I didn't have to lie anymore to them even though my mother was in complete and utter denial.

"Oh my son? He's so busy with school, he can't have a girlfriend!"

"He hasn't found the right girl yet."

"He's focusing on his studies, so he's not ready to meet a girl right now."

I came to understand that the process of acceptance was a long one for her and those were issues she had to deal with herself. However, I promised myself that when I came out to my family, I would be active in the queer community and give back to it, so I joined various groups. T.E.A.C.H. was one of these groups and it gave me confidence that helped me through the process of making myself visible as a gay person and, more specifically, as a gay Filipino. I had hoped other young queer and questioning Filipinos could see that there was more than just the color white in the community. I wanted to show the diversity of the Filipino queer community and it didn't just have hairdressers, drag queens and Avon cosmetic salespeople.

✦✦

I remember the many changes that have happened in the last seven years. I moved out on my own, graduated from university, dated people and had serious relationships, even found love a couple of times. However, nothing could have changed me more than meeting a wonderful man named Tim. This is one of those examples of love smacking you in the face when you least expect it. We were introduced by a friend and from the beginning got along really well. Tim told me the challenging life that he led and how he had to overcome adversity. For example, he had been in a car accident, which broke his back, almost paralyzing him. He got up and walked again! I was amazed by his will, his courage and his strength, and I admired that he wouldn't let anything get him down. Then, as if the accident weren't enough, he was diagnosed with cancer and told he had only a few weeks to live. Despite those odds, he went through chemotherapy and within a few months, this amazing man beat his cancer into remission.

We dated for a couple of weeks and were inseparable. I finally told him that we would be a great couple and that we should date exclusively. He agreed with me, but told me that he couldn't. I was shocked! I asked him why and he gave me one lame reason after another. Needless to say I wasn't impressed. But I pushed him, rebutted all his reasons and told him to take a chance on me, and after much cajoling (even though I'd like to think it was my charm that did it), Tim said yes to me. I would later find out that he was only making up excuses that day because he had concerns about his health. When we met, Tim had only been in remission for three and a half years; to be defined as cured, your cancer has to be in remission for five years. He wanted to be free from cancer before sharing his life with someone like me.

We took some major steps in our relationship within a short period of time. Over a few months, he met my brothers and my parents. By this time my mother was finally starting to come to terms with my sexuality, but I know my entire family liked Tim. Six months later, I officially moved in with him and we lived happily ever after ... sort of.

✦✦

I remember making plans to celebrate our one-year anniversary. We were supposed to go see a musical. However, Tim was feeling sick leading up to the date; so sick that he had to check into the hospital. What started out as extreme pain in his back due to arthritis turned out to be a serious bowel infection. For five days, the hospital ran tests to see what was causing this problem. Then we got the news: What Tim feared in the beginning of our relationship had become a reality. In only six more months he would have been considered cured, but the cancer was back. This time it was deadly bone cancer. Tim, being the person that he was, didn't complain or feel sorry for himself. He said that it was just another bump on the road and that it was time to fight again. The difference this time was that someone who loved him dearly was right there to fight with him. So the chemotherapy began and with it short stays at home and long stays in the hospital.

During Tim's battle, a huge event happened in Ontario. Gays and lesbians were allowed to marry! We had talked about having a commitment ceremony but when the courts ruled in favor of gays and lesbians, our conversations switched to getting married. We were confident that Tim would fight off this cancer again, so we planned to do the ceremony when he was in remission. He always said that the one thing he wanted to experience was being able to sit in our matching rocking chairs as senior citizens and watch the sunset (I think there were ideas of having a bevy of cute boys serving us geezers and our every whim, too, but I digress).

I remember spring and then summer and then fall, and Tim was still doing chemo. By the end of September, he began his longest stay in the hospital. Though positive through everything, he knew that things were not looking promising. Unfortunately, the doctor had to tell us that there wasn't much more treatment that Tim could do because the chemo would end up killing him. She recommended that if we wanted to get married to do it as soon as we could. Our original plan was to have the ceremony at the hospital in two weeks, but the doctor said that we should get married even sooner. Organizing a wedding is hard enough in two years; in two weeks even more so, but in our case we had to organize one in two days.

We managed to pull it off. With the help of the staff at the hospital and our close friends, we had the actual ceremony performed in Tim's hospital room by a United Church minister with our immediate family witnessing on October 18. The reception followed in the hospital conference room with about seventy of our closest friends and staff from the hospital. I look at pictures taken that day and see how happy we both were despite the odds. I see the picture of my parents smiling, specifically of my mother smiling, so proud to see her gay son married to a wonderful man like Tim.

✦✦

I remember November 1st, All Saints' Day, two weeks to the day after our wedding. This was the day that my beloved Tim passed away. The doctors and nurses were convinced he survived an extra week because he was so happy after our wedding, but they were all surprised nonetheless that his death came so suddenly and without warning. Everyone was prepared, but at the same time not prepared. I honestly think that people didn't expect Tim to die since he had overcome so much before, but a person's body can only take so much before being weakened to a point of not being able to fight any longer. Tim's death has given me the unique distinction of being a gay widower at twenty-seven.

A few weeks after the funeral, because of the pressure of Tim's passing and having to deal with lawyers and the estate, I was on the edge of an emotional breakdown. I felt like I was going to break in half because I was carrying this bag of bricks on my shoulders. I was having lunch with my mother, who was giving me advice on dealing with the estate. My mother sensed my gloominess and despair and needed to know what was wrong with me. So we ended up talking about my life and me being gay. This was a first for my mother and me, and I believe that the events with Tim really made her see that I was happy with my life and that there was nothing to be ashamed of. I remember my mother telling me during that talk that if anyone said anything bad about her gay son that she would make sure that they got a piece of her mind. As usual, I was stunned into silence, but I reflect back to when I came out to my parents and see how much my mother has progressed since that fateful day. In essence, this is not only my coming out story, but also my mother's coming out story, the story of her coming out as having a gay son.

I remember my mother saying, *"You just have to marry a good woman!"*

You're sort of right, ma. Her name was Tim.

Glossary of Terms

Bisexual — someone who is attracted physically and emotionally to persons of the same and different genders, not necessarily attracted equally to both men and women and not always attracted to both men and women at the same time. Bisexuality is often thought of as a phase on the way to coming out as gay or lesbian, but for many people, being bisexual is a lifelong sexual identity.

CelebrAsian — a queer political and advocacy group for Asians of East/South-East Asian descent/ancestry; formerly known as Gay Asians Toronto.

Church and Wellesley — an intersection in downtown Toronto; it is seen as the centre of the LGBTQ community in Toronto.

Gay — a term for someone who forms physical and emotional relationships with persons of the same gender; used to refer to both men and women, but increasingly is used only to refer to men.

Harlow, Harry — an American psychologist who studied human behavior and development by observing the behavior of primates. He is influential in general and child psychology, particularly for his research on learning, motivation and affection.

Heterosexism — the assumption that everyone is, or should be, heterosexual and that heterosexuality is the only normal, natural expression of sexuality; implies that heterosexuality is superior and therefore preferable to being homosexual, bisexual or transgendered.

Homophobia — fear and hatred of gays and lesbians expressed as prejudice, discrimination, harassment and acts of violence; kinds of homophobia include internalized homophobia — self-hatred by gays and lesbians who grow up internalizing the prejudices of the straight world around them — and institutional homophobia (e.g., denying housing or employment to a person who is gay or lesbian). Violence against transsexual and transgendered people is known as transphobia. Homophobia and transphobia are not just experienced by people who are gay or lesbian but by people who are thought to be gay or lesbian because they do not necessarily fit in with assigned gender roles; for example, women who have short hair or dress in a certain way may be called "dykes."

Lesbian — a woman whose primary emotional and sexual attraction is to women; many form physical and emotional relationships with other women.

LGBTOUT — Lesbians, Gays, Bisexuals and Transgendered of the University of Toronto, the officially recognized group at the University of Toronto for lesbian, gay, bisexual, transgendered, transsexual, queer students and others who are marginalized on the basis of their sexual orientations and/or gender identifications; LGBTOUT has been fighting for queer rights and visibility for more than thirty years!

LGBTQ — lesbian, gay, bisexual, trans, queer.

LGBYT — Lesbian, Gay, Bisexual Youth of Toronto, the former name of the group now known as WAVE; the Toronto-based youth group holds weekly support group meetings for youth who do not identify as straight.

OAC — Ontario Academic Credits; until 2003, this was the fifth year of high school in the province of Ontario, used to prepare students for university; admission into most Ontario universities required six OAC credits.

Queen West — a number of Toronto neighborhoods along trendy Queen Street West, which is lined with shops, restaurants, cafés and galleries.

Rule, Jane — an American-born lesbian and feminist writer, who moved to Canada in 1956, teaching at the University of British Columbia until 1976; she has written a number of works, including *Desert of the Heart* (1964) and *After the Fire* (1989).

School's Out — a National Film Board of Canada film directed by Lynne Fernie featuring volunteers from T.E.A.C.H. talking about their experiences as anti-homophobia educators; also features Jane Rule.

SEC — University of Toronto's Sexual Education and Peer Counselling Centre; the center provides resources and information, counseling and a telephone hotline, regarding all aspects of human sexuality.

Transgendered — a self-identifying term for someone whose gender identity or expression differs from traditional gender roles; also a political umbrella term in English-speaking North America used to refer to everyone who crosses gender roles in one way or another, including transsexuals, drag queens, transvestites, etc.

Transsexual — someone whose gender identity is different from the biological gender that they were assigned to at birth. A transsexual person might change gender by having surgery known as gender assignment surgery, take hormones, or do electrolysis; this process of changes is known as transitioning. Transsexuals can be transmen, female-to-male (FTM), or transwomen, male-to-female (MTF). Transmen generally use male pronouns and transwomen generally use female pronouns. Trans people may identify as gay, lesbian, straight or bisexual. At the simplest level, a transsexual can be explained as a boy who wants to be a girl or a girl who wants to be a boy.

Two-spirited — a term for First Nations peoples who are lesbian, gay, bisexual, transgendered or transsexual; it refers particularly to gender. Two-spirited people had positive and elevated status among many aboriginal nations prior to the arrival of Europeans.

U of T — University of Toronto.

The 519 or the **519 Community Centre** — a community center located at 519 Church Street in downtown Toronto, with a focus on the LGBTQ community; more than three hundred groups use the 519 for meeting space, providing services and other programs for the diverse community.

✦✦✦

Contributor Biographies

j.t.s. berrigan — j.t.s. berrigan is a Black, queer educator who has lived in Toronto since 1999. With familial connections in Canada's east coast, the West Indies and other spaces, he calls many places home.

njeri-damali (campbell) — njeri-damali (campbell) studies channeling, creativity, anti-oppression/resistance, popular theater and dance. She is pursuing a master's degree in education at York University and is the Executive Director of the Ontario Young People's Alliance.

Anthony Collins — Anthony is an under-focused undergrad at the University of Toronto. Books, films, good conversation, tea, politics, employment and volunteering are his most frequent excuses for not applying himself in school.

Jenn F. — Jenn was born and raised in Toronto where she successfully transitioned in 2001. Her life is full of love and laughter and she cherishes her experiences with T.E.A.C.H.

Shawn Fowler — Shawn is a longtime, former T.E.A.C.H. volunteer. He currently works at Planned Parenthood of Toronto and is looking forward to raising Sicilian miniature donkeys in his retirement.

M. Francino — M. is a self-identified (for what it's worth), queer, white francophone born in English Canada, a pre-operative FTM on testosterone who is attending university and has been with T.E.A.C.H. for two years. Long live drag and activism!

ayden isak hoffman-scheim — ayden "andy" isak hoffman-scheim is a seventeen-year-old radical dropout, educator, survivor and dreamer. He works with queer and trans youth doing art and revolution, cooks, learns and makes plans for overthrowing the gender binary.

Amina Jabbar — Amina Jabbar is currently a student in social work at Ryerson University. She has been volunteering with T.E.A.C.H. for three and a half years.

Johan Kim — Johan, a twenty-year-old student at the University of Toronto, joined T.E.A.C.H. two years ago. He is a Queerean (queer + Korean) and proud of his heritage. A volunteer with numerous organizations ranging from international development to anti-homophobia, Johan strives to make or break the world.